Review

"This is a gem of a book! As someone
both personally and as a tool for m
enough to think I've got a handle on social media but this book
has shown me there's so much more to learn. I'll no doubt
return to this again and again."
Grant Stott, TV and Radio Presenter

"One of the most clear and compelling guides ever
published for what works in social media, and why.
Highly recommended!"
**Jay Baer, founder of Convince & Convert and
author of Hug Your Haters**

"Finally, a book about business that I actually want to read.
Packed full of useful stuff, and entertaining too. A must
for anyone already working in social media, or anyone
considering making a career out of it."
**Helena Langdon, Stand-Up Comedian and
Former Head of Digital at Innocent**

"An enjoyable read that will motivate you to embrace social
media platforms. This book is a winner and a great asset to
anybody who is ambitious about growing their brand."
**Kieron Achara, GB Olympian and
Mental Health Ambassador**

"Engaging and informative and so important now as many
businesses have been forced to move online to promote their
services. This book provides so many good reasons about why
and how to do that successfully."
**Laura Irvine, Specialist in Data Protection Law, and
Partner at Davidson Chalmers Stewart**

"This book clears the noise allowing you and your business to focus. Packed with great tips, tools, case studies, and insight, these guys have done a lot of the hard work for you!"
Joanna Steele, Director, Dimax Digital Ltd

"Fun, engaging and thought-provoking content to help your business. We have witnessed our members grow their customer base applying Gary and Colin's digital teachings over the last decade – now you can too. A must read."
Bob Grant, Chief Executive,
Renfrewshire Chamber of Commerce

"I hate social media and spend way too much time on it. This book makes me want to spend even more time on it. But get better at it. I don't know what to feel about this!"
Gavin Oattes, Author and Inspirational Speaker

"This book has something for everyone, whether you're just beginning to embrace social media for business or you use it day in day out and think you have it all sussed already! Funny, honest and full of genuinely great advice."
Laurie Findlay, Director of Training Matters Ltd

"Entertaining and witty, this book engages the reader yet still manages to give clear focus on all aspects of social media. I am so impressed with how much relevant guidance and inspiration they have stuffed in between the covers that I plan on asking all staff to read it too."
Laura McAlpine, Director and
Principal Optometrist, Opticare Opticians

"A cracking read! Perfectly pitched for the small business with lots of useful tips and tricks and real life examples of how to improve social media presence."
Stuart McKenna, CEO at
Scottish Training Federation Limited

"embrace the space"

Inspirational insight from a decade of delivering social media training to businesses that give a damn!

GARY ENNIS & COLIN KELLY

NS

Published by NSDesign Ltd
Registered Address:
22 Montrose Street,
Merchant City, Glasgow, G1 1RE
Telephone: 0141 737 0178
Website: www.nsdesign.co.uk

© Gary Ennis & Colin Kelly

Copyright Notice
Our lawyer, Big Claire, sent us half a page of A4 to include here.
A load of stuff about reserving all our rights and other legal-speak
we don't really understand or care about. The truth is we actually
WANT you to share this stuff; screenshite parts of it, Tweet bits
you enjoy, pass it round your friends, use the good bits in
training you run or speeches or conferences or whatever.
But if you try to pass any of it off as your own work, sell it yourself,
or generally take the piss, that's not OK and we'll be sending her
round. If you're sharing anything that includes an illustration from
this book, then you should credit www.keithatherton.com.
We're very grateful to Keith for his work and he's bigger than
both of us. We also think Big Claire is pretty keen on him.
Run Keith, RUUUUNNNNNNN!!!!!!!

The moral right of the author has been asserted.
A catalogue record for this book is available from
the British Library

ISBN: 978-1-83813-500-3

Illustrated by Keith Atherton
Designed by Melvin Creative Ltd
Edited by Melanie Sims

Printed and bound in the EU

"embrace the space"

.

Dedication

From Gary

To Jan, Josh and Jamie. Who not only support me in everything I do, but challenge me to do it better. Always x.

From Colin

To Emma and the boys. You can achieve anything you put your mind to.

From both of us

Firstly, to all the businesses we've ever worked with. We can't name you all, but you know who you are. To the organisations large and small who've put their trust in us to deliver training programmes, support your clients, coach your staff, set up your profiles, design your strategies, write your policies and even post on your behalf. We hope you've learned half as much from us, as we've learned from you. Without you, this book wouldn't exist.

Next up, a special shout out to the NSDesign team, past and present. Every one of us 'Digital Champions' dedicated to making a real difference in everything we do.

And finally, a huge thanks to you. Yes you – the person right now reading this book. This book is dedicated to you, because you know digital can help your business grow.

You're right, so keep reading.

Blame Bon Jovi

If you've bought this book and you don't enjoy it – blame Bon Jovi. Seriously, it's Jon and the gang's fault (and that includes Richie Sambora and maybe even Alec John Such[1]), so speak to them if you want a refund.

Why? Well without Bon Jovi, Gary would never have met Colin. In short, a chance radio competition, some bad singing of Keep the Faith, some follow on fun and banter (which involved taking Colin's head on a stick to the concert), and the rest is part history, part folklore[2].

As for Keith (our amazing illustrator), Gary was meant to spend three days with him delivering business consultancy a few years ago. Instead they spent three days discussing the entire Bon Jovi back catalogue. Amazingly Keith never asked for his money back!

---

[1] Maybe by the time you read this, Jon and Richie will have kissed and made up and the band will be back to its best. No offence Alec, but it ain't ever happening.
[2] If you absolutely must know more - take a listen here: https://bit.ly/etsbook-howgarymetcolin

Foreword

It's about bloody time Gary and Colin wrote this book. Having known them for years, and having seen them in action many times, they are beyond doubt two of the biggest champions of digital in Scotland and beyond. They know their stuff. Trust me – I pinch loads of it for my own talks! I've been lucky to get a peek at the pages which follow. You're in for a treat: with real insight from the front line of social media, delivered in a way that only they can.

I've Embraced The Space. You will too. Hold on tight...

Stephen Whitelaw, Digital Consultant and Speaker

Looking Forward

Ok, we've had the foreword, now let's crack on by *looking forward* (did you see what I did there?). Looking forward to when social media isn't quite the lifeline that it has suddenly become.

In March 2020 the world changed. The global pandemic that is COVID-19 (still causing mayhem at the time of writing) literally caused the world to hit the pause button. This book was approximately 80% written at the time, and while throughout it you'll see that we advocate the use of digital technologies, nobody could quite have seen the impending absolute requirement of them.

Overnight, every business became a technology business.

Shops forced to close, scrambled to open up ecommerce websites. Corporate teams who once met in person round the boardroom table, suddenly had to work out remote video conferencing via Zoom from their newly created home offices. And every small business owner on the planet (once the initial panic had resided) turned to social media, looking for a way to talk to customers, staff, friends and family. Not just as an alternative route to market, but to show a human side.

Kindness, empathy, compassion, generosity, care, reassurance, honesty – all human traits that right now cannot be shown face to face, and instead are being communicated via Facebook, Instagram, LinkedIn, TikTok, Twitter and more. It's not quite the same, but I hate to think what the negative impact on our mental health might be if we didn't have access to these social platforms, which only recently were often being cited as negative influences on our well-being.

Technology is rarely the cause of significant change but it's often one of the answers to getting you through it. So to paraphrase Darwin, as Leon Meggison did:

> **66** It is not the strongest of the species that survives, nor the most intelligent that survives. It is the one that is most adaptable to change. **99**

Businesses have had no option but to change recently. Those businesses which were already embracing social media will probably do a little better than those which saw it as an inconvenience, or worse, a fad. If the impact of a COVID-19 lockdown hasn't been enough to convince you of the need to grab these technologies with both hands, and see how they can help you stand out for all the right reasons at this time of global change, then I'd politely ask you to put this book back down on the shelf and we'll call it quits.

Social Media is here to stay: I'd have started this book with such a sentiment regardless of the impact from any global pandemic. I suggest you embrace it (maybe more than ever right now), but I also look forward to when we can chat again in person, not via Facebook Messenger, or through our webcams on a training webinar, but instead socially over coffee and biscuits (which to confirm, Colin's buying!).

Contents

Introduction 17

01 It's not all just cat videos 25
(but you should probably still make some)

02 The golden rules of success on social media 33
(and why sharing is caring)

03 The social platforms explained 43
(with some help from a teenager)

04 The dreaded social media algorithms 85
(and why it's no longer just a numbers game)

05 How to beat the algorithms 93
(with some knock-out engagement tactics)

06 Creating great content 107
(which stands out from the crowd)

07 Live streaming, webinars and video conferencing 117
(and why digital 'face to face' still matters)

08 Paid social media 125
(and why most businesses do it wrong)

09 Social customer service 133
(and our 'famous' 3 B's)

10 Ratings, reviews and recommendations 145
(and encouraging your customers to do your marketing for you)

11 The rise of the social media influencer 155
(and how to get the most for your money if using one)

12 Tone of voice 161
(and developing your brand personality)

13 Social media dangers 175
(and staying on the right side of the law)

14 Cyber security 191
(and the steps to protect against anti-social behaviour)

15 Learning from the data 207
(and why you should never measure hits)

16 Social media in the mainstream media 213
(and how to grab headlines in the real world)

17 Why your website still matters 221
(and the importance of blogging)

18 Viral videos 231
(with some nostalgic advice from a cat)

19 Before you go: Dinosaur or Dodo? 243
(probably neither because you're reading this)

20 Bonus chapters 247

About the authors 275

Epilogue 281

Introduction

by Gary

Social media.

Two words which rarely (if ever) appeared beside each other prior to the millennium, but which are now as commonly used as sliced bread (not that I can ever remember the words 'sliced bread' being used anywhere, other than on the side of the packaging for sliced bread).

Two words which elicit different responses from people when you ask them (as we regularly do) to describe what the phrase means to them. From 'The Devil's spawn' and 'An evil necessity' to 'The future of communication' and 'Just the way we talk', these two words split public opinion more than Brexit, with some championing its democracy and ability to bring together communities for positive benefit, while others complain about its anti-social nature, its addictive qualities, and its contribution to the demise of face to face conversation.

No matter your personal opinion, what arguably cannot be disputed is the impact of social media on businesses. With billions[3] of people using the various platforms and channels (many of which we'll discuss later on) it's now almost impossible for business owners to ignore the likes of Facebook and Instagram as a means to reach new and existing customers, not just for marketing purposes, but for product support, sales, customer service and more.

Social media is here to stay. It's not a fad or a flash in the pan; it's as credible a business opportunity as your website, shop window, rolodex[4], CRM[5] system, sales team and more (I'd argue even more important, but then I'm biased), and to quote Erik Qualman, a respected social media guru from America:

❝ We don't have a choice on whether we DO social media, the question is how well we DO it.[6] **❞**

I agree – you really don't have a choice. Your customers, your staff, and your competitors are all using it, and you need to use it too, and use it well. Just

---

[3] Note that throughout this book, we'll try and not quote any exact figures. That way it won't look immediately out of date when you're reading it, and the numbers are all significantly higher!
[4] Careful - If you didn't have to Google 'Rolodex' then you're showing your age.
[5] Apologies for the TLA (three letter acronym) - we'll try and avoid as much geeky jargon as we can. Technically - CRM is not an acronym, it's an initialism, but we can argue about that in person in the future (otherwise we risk the footnotes in this book being longer than the book itself).
[6] More from Erik Qualman on his blog: https://bit.ly/etsbook-equalman

being on Facebook is no longer enough; being there with business intent, reason, purpose, strategy, might begin to deliver some results for you. You don't have a phone on your desk just to randomly call people, you use it to make a difference, and the social platforms are no different. Just as I would expect you to answer the phone if I ring your office number, I expect you to respond to my tweet, post, or comment on social media; that's just basic courtesy. However, in today's always-connected world, I expect a whole lot more. The businesses which help me, inspire me, educate and entertain me on social media – those are the businesses I want to do business with (and I'll be telling my 338[7] friends about them too).

Do none of that and you're just another business, trying to reach me on dormant platforms, trading on your past, and fast at risk of becoming a dinosaur. Or a dodo. I'll explain the difference later on, but let's just say for now that neither are relevant in today's business world.

Social media. And you thought it was all just cat videos.

Firstly - what is this book?

Short of telling you that it's a collection of 287 sheets of paper bound on one side, allowing you to open it, flip through the pages one by one, and stop when you run out, we'd like to offer a short explanation of what this book actually is, and how best to read this book based on your own current circumstances. I'm hoping that you've already bought it, so that if by the end of this section, you're thinking 'nope, not for me', then too late, we've already got your money, and you've a nice shiny new book on your shelf[8] (next to all the other ones you bought but haven't got round to reading).

This book is based on the learnings and experiences from over a decade of running social media training workshops. Specifically, our Embrace The Space business masterclass which Colin and I have now delivered to over 10,000 businesses across the UK.

---

[7] https://bit.ly/etsbook-howmanyfriends
[8] Or a perfect doorstop. Seriously - at 287 pages long, we've done the research - this book should make an ideal doorstop if you'd rather use it in a more functional manner - we're all about the multi-purpose!

We've been there from the early days of everyone simply wanting to know 'what is social media?' and 'should we use it?', to the mass adoption of the platforms, the change in public attitudes, and the challenges it has posed to business as it evolved. Having been in many rooms with organisations of all shapes and sizes – them learning from us, us learning from them – and the sharing and discussion that we have facilitated, we like to think that the Embrace The Space masterclasses are some of the best business workshops out there (If Carlsberg did social media training...).

This book aims to encapsulate what makes the workshops so special.

It's first and foremost a book to help businesses achieve more through social media. Advice, tips, best practice, personal ramblings, gut feelings and more – all with the aim of trying to help you (and your organisation) get to grips with the likes of Facebook, Instagram, LinkedIn etc. – and more importantly, see a business benefit from them.

It's also a chance for Colin and I to get nostalgic. To share fun stories and relevant examples because if we don't commit them to print soon, our brains will filter them out as we run out of data storage. While far from autobiographical, there are elements in these pages which might give you an insight into both of us, our attitudes, styles[9] and the businesses we've run. People often tell us that it's our 'on-stage' relationship that makes Embrace The Space so unique, so we'll try and convey a bit of that as well (without getting too bromance on you).

Some chapters you'll see are written by me (the ones which mock Colin, and have a tendency for gratuitous use of footnotes), some by Colin (the ones which mock me, and utilise a far more professional writing style: he has to make use of that Journalism degree somehow), and some are a mix from us both, as our two mindsets begin to meld (and when we couldn't think of any jokes at the other's expense).

It seems to work well in person, so we're hoping it translates ok in book form!

---

[9] Not obviously our fashion styles - there will be no pictures showing you what we have worn throughout the years. If there's a demand for this type of thing, let me know and I'll register geektrainerapparal.com straight away.

Who this book is for

This book is arguably for anyone in business. Specifically, it's been written (as have the workshops over the years) for people within small and medium businesses who actually give a damn. People who care about how their business performs. People who care about the relationship they have with customers; whether running their own business, or working for someone else.

If you've ever sat in front of your Facebook business page on a Friday and thought, 'Jings it's Friday, we've said nothing all week, I better say something', then this book is especially for you. If you're struggling with what to say, which platform to say it on, and why to bother in the first place – again, this is for you. And if you're banging your head against the desk wondering how to achieve more sales, better customer advocacy, increased positive PR, and more impact from your use of social media – then keep reading!

This book is not a technical guidebook. It will not show you how to 'do Facebook' (or indeed any of the popular social platforms). It won't dig into technical details (other than a few exceptions) about the practical mechanics of LinkedIn or Instagram. And it won't (by a long shot) be the only book you need to read to ensure success for your business on social media.

This book should be considered food for thought. Especially because much of it, we know from experience, isn't actually thought about; certainly not as much as it maybe should be.

How to read it

Go all in, block out eight hours (that's how long it will probably take) and read this cover to cover, checking out the various websites and resources along the way.

Or feel free to jump in at any chapter that you think will help right now. Got an issue with customer service? Jump straight to Chapter 9 for a steer on how social media can help. Trying to get to grips with TikTok? Then head to Chapter 3 where we'll tell you what we think about it. Each chapter has been designed to stand on its own, allowing you to dip in accordingly.

Alternatively, you may just decide on the 'I've got ten minutes and need to pretend I know all about this stuff' route. We've got your back, and suggest you quickly read all the 'Chapter in a tweet' summaries. These offer very quick breakdowns of the key points from each chapter. If you only read these gems then you're entitled to add 'Social Media Guru' to your CV immediately. Trust me, others have done so on much less!

Lastly, if you're really up for a challenge, you could just read the footnotes and nothing else. If you do, please contact me afterwards and tell me what you thought the book was about.

Regardless of how you choose to read this, a quick final tip about some of the 'extras' in the book.

#TrainerLife – These short anecdotes will hopefully give you an insight into the life of a busy trainer. We've seen it all over the years, and have the scars to prove it. We'll share some of our own memorable moments for your amusement.

!GeekAlert – We'll try not to give you too much geek speak, but occasionally (where relevant) we'll sneak in a weblink, or some details about something quite technical. For the record, I'm a geek and proud of it, but I realise not everyone wants to talk about pixel sizes or bounce rates. Where we go all geeky on you, we'll warn you in advance, and it'll be worth it[10].

*Case Study – To help reinforce some of our chat, we'll introduce actual case studies relevant to the chapter topic. Real businesses with real challenges, most of which we've worked with in some shape or form over the years. Thanks in advance to the businesses who gave us permission to talk openly about them.

Consider this book a conversation starter. And like any good chat, we'd be delighted if you replied and kept the conversation going. There's some

---

[10] I just did a 'hair flick'.

more information (including contact details) on both of us at the end of the book, but you'll not be surprised to hear we're easily found on most social media platforms too. Drop by and say hello, or post up your own thoughts using the #ETSbook hashtag.

Unless of course you want a refund.

!GeekAlert

Social media is an area within 'digital marketing' and just one sign of a general shift towards significantly more 'digital' activity in recent years.

Have a look at The Internet Minute from Lori Lewis (Twitter: @lorilewis) for a powerful visualisation of how busy the digital space is becoming and a stark reminder of how hard it is now for anyone to cut through the noise and get any sort of attention.

SCAN ME[11]

---

[11] You didn't think we'd write a book and not have some clever offline/online crossover thing going on! Just in case you've no idea what this is - it's a QR-Code. Rather than explain what they are, we hope you work it out. There's one for every chapter, so get your phone out and point your camera at it. Have fun!

01

It's not all just cat videos

(but you should probably still make some)

Gary

It's safe to say that one of my least favourite phrases over the last ten years plus has been 'Social Media Marketing'.

It infers that social media is JUST marketing. That it's just about promotions, campaigns, advertising, and selling. It's true that marketing is about way more than those things, but when you precede marketing with social media, most people (including business owners) think about making money, sponsored adverts, and having the next big viral video – most of them involving cats!

I'm not telling you not to make cat videos (indeed, keep reading and I'll explain why you should make cat videos), but I'm warning you about treating social media purely as a marketing channel. Maybe back at the start of the millennium (when social was new and shiny) it was exactly that, but things have definitely moved on. Now social media is very much embedded into people's everyday lives. It's not where they go to be marketed to but where they go to chat, to catch up with friends, to be entertained, to live. And (at the risk of sounding ageist) the younger the user, the more embedded in their lives it is.

This was brilliantly confirmed at one of our workshops a few years ago when we asked the audience (as we always do) 'What is Social Media?'[12]. We had a father and son with us that day. Their respective responses still make us laugh today:

The father – a typical example of a middle-aged businessman, attending in shirt and tie – was resistant to the idea of his business messing around on Facebook (where his kids are spending too much time, and getting into bother), but was willing to consider it if it could make him money.

The son – a late teen – just gets on and uses it to engage with friends, family, brands he admires, celebrities, and more. Fun because it is. With silly friends photos, daft jokes, internet memes, and cat videos littered throughout his news feed on a daily basis.

---

[12] We start most workshops asking this question. We've had some memorable answers over the years: https://bit.ly/etsbook-whatissocial

Whether you like it or not, social media is now part of everyday life. Some would say it's now far too embedded into people's daily routines, and there's no doubt that serious issues around addiction, online bullying, and self-worth exist today in part because of Facebook and the other social tools people use to express their worst attitudes. This book will conveniently 'sit on the fence' when it comes to these issues; not because we don't think they're important (quite the opposite – with both Colin and myself having young families who will be influenced more by social media than ever before), but because there are better more qualified advisors for this than us [13].

This is, after all, a book to help businesses. And when we do discuss the dangers around social media (covered in Chapter 13) we'll tend to keep them related to the business dangers.

Back to marketing......Try this test: ask your friends, your staff, or your work colleagues to open up Facebook on their mobile phone[14] and to show you the last thing they engaged with. That is, the last bit of content they either liked, commented on, or shared. On the assumption they play along (and

---

[13] 'Left To Their Own Devices' by Katharine Hill is one such example that I'd encourage any parent to read asap!
[14] Worth noting that most people use Facebook (and most other social platforms) via the mobile app on their smart phone. At the time of writing 98% of all users consume Facebook's content on a screen measuring approx 2 inches wide - we'll remind you of this again later when it comes to creating effective content.

aren't too embarrassed to show you), the chances are that content will be something fun.

It's not just the youngsters. We all 'like' our best pal's holiday photos. Many of us will comment (often without thinking) on the daft 'Can you name an animal beginning with E that isn't an elephant?' questions posed (or shared) by our friends. And who can't resist watching, if not sharing (because it's that funny!) the cute video of the baby kitten chasing the laser pointer.

If we're honest about it, the bulk of our social media usage is daft, pointless, harmless fun: the lighter side of life. It's me procrastinating, browsing nonsense when I probably should be getting on with other stuff. And just to confirm – that's FINE!

What people are not engaging with on any regular basis are businesses which market themselves. Businesses which sell, promote, advertise and spam. Look at your own feed (and you're a respected professional person after all, right?) when was the last time you liked a business post? When was the last time you thought, 'Wow, great end of year results from Scotrail, my friends will love this' and clicked 'share'? When was the last time you shared anything of a commercial nature from a business marketing themselves on social media?

It's not a common occurrence is it? And it's not just uncommon for you. All these businesses seduced by social media marketing, with billions of potential customers all pretty much ignoring their content[15].

Of course there are exceptions. Of course there are some businesses and organisations with which you do regularly engage. Consider these examples:

1. Your favourite sports team, your children's school, your partner's small business. All of them organisations that connect with you on a personal level. Because they mean something. When was the last time any other type of business said something truly meaningful to you? That had you

---

[15] Sometimes they're not ignoring it - often they simply don't see it. We'll cover this later when we discuss the impact of the social media algorithm.

desperate to share their content because of how relevant, personal, and valuable it was to you (and therefore your friends, family and/or peers would benefit too).

2. There are also exceptions based on you engaging with companies in ways they'd prefer you didn't. I'm not proud of it, but I too (like many) have been a 'social media ranter'!. Using Twitter to tag in a train company to have a go at them about yet another late train. Or hijacking the latest promotional post from your Satellite TV provider to tell them to 'Shove the latest boxset where the sun don't shine, and please refund me the payment you illegally took from me'[16].

3. The final exception is when you engage with businesses because they're NOT marketing to you. Their post is not overly promotional, an obvious advert, or purely for their benefit, but yours. Even better if the post (as we've just discussed) is actually meaningful. Personal. Funny. A business which posts content in similar ways your friends do. Content designed to make you laugh, cry, think, and keep you entertained. Companies which post cat videos.

Please be aware that when I suggest 'Cat video' content, I'm not always being literal. I once did some consultancy with a particular Scottish local authority whose content was simply not engaging with the local audience they were trying to attract. I encouraged them to make cat videos. The following week they proudly showed me the two cat videos posted to their feed.

Cat videos are daft, silly, fun, light hearted, and they make (most people) smile. It's perfect 'online content' that people like to waste time consuming, and will often share with their friends. You don't need to make cat videos, but I'd urge you to consider what your version of that is. Where are your funny stories, your images which humanise the brand, and the #fail examples from your industry which make people engage with you. Stop trying to sell me your ladders, and share that funny link of '100 idiots who fell off ladders'. Now I'm smiling. Now I'm sharing your content. Now I'm thinking ladders. Now I'm aware of you. Marketing done.

---

[16] All fictitious examples I stress. Honestly I never said them.

66 When dealing with people, let us remember we are not dealing with creatures of logic. We are dealing with creatures of emotion. **99**
Dale Carnegie, How to Win Friends and Influence People

Don't get me wrong, effective social media for businesses isn't just posting silly videos and memes all day every day. There's so much more to social than cat videos. But it's a pretty good place to start, especially if you're honest with yourself, look at your own content, and admit, 'not even I'd share that'. So why would a customer?

*Case Study: The Power of Fun

Two organisations which we often flag up as truly understanding the value in making an audience smile are Orkney Library and Innocent Smoothies. Poles apart in terms of what they do, who their market is, and the budgets available to them, but having had the pleasure of speaking to the people 'behind the tweets', their social strategies are strikingly similar.

Orkney Library's primary purpose (like most local libraries) is to promote reading, and provide books to the community. But that doesn't mean they can't have one of the biggest personalities on the Internet! Just because every other public sector library sounds and looks like a public sector library, doesn't mean they need to follow the herd. The truth is, on social media, all the other libraries want to be just like Orkney, but haven't got the guts (or maybe the management backing?) to break from the norm and let their hair down.

Regular content includes their #BookFace photo mashups, their stories of 'Booky McBookFace', and their 'Balls Report'. You'd be surprised how much fun and entertainment can be extracted from telling people about books.

In their words: "It's really not rocket science. The humour brings them in, which allows us to get the important information across". And it certainly does get them in, with over 70K followers on Twitter, they are one of the most followed libraries on the planet.

Fly 529 miles south from Kirkwall and you'll reach London – home of Innocent Smoothies. A household brand across the UK and beyond, this fruit juice smoothie company is synonymous with fun, through their quirky logo and silly jokes on their drinks packaging. They're also the only company I know whose white delivery vans are actually green, because they're covered top to bottom in fake grass. Certainly turns heads driving up the M6.

Just like Orkney Library they know they 'stand out' on the social channels. With a cheeky, fun, sometimes weird and wonderful attitude to marketing, their #DogsAtPollingStations or #PenguinAwarenessDay campaigns might not immediately sell additional fruit drinks, but they massively help to build customer relationships, and makes Innocent truly memorable.

We were lucky to catch up with Innocent's Head of Digital, Helena Langdon, a few years back who gave us an insight into how they approach things: "We've always been a social brand. Way before Facebook and everything else, we've been trying to have a two-way dialogue with customers at every opportunity. Social media just gives us a license to talk about whatever we want. Not just about the product, or rambling musings, but about things going on in the world, where we have an opportunity to say something about it which might resonate with people. Our ethos is to keep it personal. Talk to humans like a human, not like a brand. Invest in nonsense conversations. Nonsense works. Never underestimate the power of nonsense!"[17]

CHAPTER IN A TWEET

Social Media. For most people it's a platform to procrastinate, share silly memes, chat to friends, and watch cat videos. The clue is in the title. It's 'SOCIAL' media. Not spam me media. Not force your business crap on me media. Join in, have fun and actually BE social!

---

[17] Want more from Helena? Watch her fantastic talk at 'Working Digital'- a conference we hosted in Ayrshire in 2018 - https://bit.ly/etsbook-helenalangdon

02

The golden rules of success on social media

(and why sharing is caring)

Colin

The amount of grey hair on Gary's head is testament to the fact that, for some, social media can become overwhelming. (And he's someone who actually likes this stuff!)

There are so many platforms, so many ways of getting a message to the world, so many feeds and algorithms, strategies and tactics that there comes a point where all you want to do is run away and scream.

Very few of us got into this with the sole intention of 'doing' social media. Most photographers I know would rather spend their time walking dogs than staring at Facebook's news feed. And most dog walkers I know would much rather be footering around with the latest expensive camera than figuring out how to set up an RSS feed in Hootsuite.

The eagle-eyed among you might have spotted a small error in that last paragraph. If you did, well done. You've a greater attention to detail than our proofreader who will now be fired.

Three golden rules

We have a simple, foolproof, easy to follow technique to STOP social media driving you round the bend. We've taken everything we know about this stuff, everything we've learned from the hundreds of businesses we've worked with over the years, all the other stuff we've soaked up from the gurus and the think tanks, and condensed it all into three simple rules for success, which I'm going to share with you now.

Our entire approach is underpinned by these three rules, and they're dead simple. I'll tell you what they are and then explain them in more detail but they're very straightforward.

Ready? Here goes.

1. Know your business
2. Know your audience
3. Give them something they want to share

Know your business

Let's explore 'Know Your Business' in more detail.

This is essential and, even if you never went near social media, it's still something you should do to give yourself any chance of success.

You (and anyone working for you) need to know what you're all about.

What is it you do? What business are you in? What makes you special? What's the point? What problems do you solve?

It's worth getting the team together, writing down some answers to this point individually and then comparing notes. You might find some gems in there or you might discover someone working with you has entirely the wrong idea about what your business actually does.

Take some time and flesh out the answers – the deeper and more specific you go the better.

Some businesses take this to quite an extreme; it keeps the founder up at night and they create slogans and mission statements and put them on the wall. You don't necessarily need to do that but please do aim to get a solid understanding of the business you're in and think about how you'd explain it all to an outsider.

Know your audience

Now we move onto 'Know Your Audience'. This is really about establishing who it is you're talking to. Customers. Potential customers. Journalists and the media. Your competitors, politicians.....people who own dogs, single mums who like holidays in France with their kids.....it could be a pretty long list. The trick here is to go really specific. So if you do have a large general audience, take time to split it up into sub-sections and really hone it down, and get to know these people in serious detail.

This exercise is one of the most important you'll ever do. Getting it right makes everything so much easier. It's not just thinking about the audience in terms of demographics (age, location, relationship status etc.) it's about moving beyond that and getting into their interests, lifestyles and then a serious look at their values.

So you might think about these questions. How much disposable income do they have? Where do they go on a Friday night? How many times a month can they afford to eat out? Do they watch X-Factor? Where do they go on holiday? Do they use Apple laptops or do they prefer PCs? Or Chromebooks? Do they commute to work? Do they use public transport? Are they likely to be vegans? How did they find out about your business?

The deeper you go, the better. The object of the exercise is to truly understand what makes your audience tick. And don't try to 'guess'. This exercise works best if you actually find out concrete answers. For some businesses, that's easier than for others. If you're a friendly local coffee shop with staff that enjoy building a rapport with customers some of them might quite naturally share some of that information with you. If you are a relatively anonymous ecommerce provider selling garden furniture via drop shipping it's going to be much harder to find that level of detail.

All I'll say is that the businesses that really make a success of this, leave nothing to chance. So consider focus groups or customer surveys. Get some of your regulars together, and perhaps some more 'casual' customers too, give them an incentive if you have to, and ask them some questions to find out who they really are.

That information is gold dust to any business serious about growth. The information alone might give you insight and ideas to refine your product offering or even reposition your business. If you've never done it, it could be really valuable.

Some businesses even build 'avatars' of their audience or their typical customer. They give them a name, create an image of them and stick them on the wall and keep them in mind every time they're communicating.

'Our typical customer is Jenny, she's 33, drives a Citroen Saxo, has a four year old son and gets out once a month to 'Shuffles' on Renfield Street.'[18]

You might not go that far but the more you understand the people you're talking to on social media the easier it's going to be to display empathy towards them which will help build rapport. If you run paid promotions and adverts, a clear understanding of who you are aiming at will help with that too.

These two exercises – Know Your Business and Know Your Audience – are worth doing every couple of years in your business. Especially if you've been through a period of change and had some personnel changes. Get the staff or the senior team together and 're-set' yourselves, establishing a focus around who you are and who you're speaking to. We live in a world with a very high pace of change and things can drift from time to time; it's worth re-establishing some focus every now and again.

Gary does this regularly with the NSDesign team. He gets everyone in the room and gets us all answering questions like 'What are we good at?', 'What are we known for?', 'Who do we inspire the most?', and 'What could we be world-class at?'. He uses the answers and the team's passion for specific topics and services to drive the business forward, sometimes taking radical steps along the way.

Give them something they want to share

Finally, Point 3 'Give them something they want to share'.

Note the words 'give them something' – it does not say 'create'. Lots of businesses make life very hard for themselves because they assume everything they publish on social media has to be something they've come up with from scratch. No wonder it becomes overwhelming!

Think about a local accountant. They could write a blog called 'Ten Ways To Save Money On Your Tax Return'. But what about the material coming out

---

[18] If Jenny actually exists she's going to be sorely disappointed because 'Shuffles' closed in 1989.

every day from HMRC with advice for small business owners? What about the Federation of Small Business? Or the local Chamber of Commerce? What are they saying on their websites or social media channels that might help the accountant's followers with their businesses? Do these organisations have expertise and information which might be of some value to the people who follow the accountant? Of course they do. And all it takes to share it is to click the 'Share' (Facebook\LinkedIn) or 'ReTweet' (Twitter) button. And that just takes a split second. And if you're a smart accountant you're probably connected to those sorts of organisations already. So the content appears in your feed and at the touch of a button you can curate it and pass it on to your followers.

Apply that to your own sector and think about quality sources of content that you can pass on to your own audience. Add in the trade journal. The BBC news website. Think geographically too: if you have customers in your community, what news and information is there that's relevant to them? Think about charity campaigns. Education, changing legislation. There's a tonne of material, already out there that you could simply pass on, establishing yourself as a valuable, reliable source and gaining credibility and followers in the process.

Remember when you share curated information you can either share it exactly as it is, or add a comment and some insight from yourself alongside it. I'd advise against curating content from a direct competitor but don't be afraid to look at businesses similar to yours abroad or even someone like you, but five years further down the line, running a bigger business with more experience. Think too about your own clients and existing customers. What news and information are they sharing today? Don't be so obsessed with growing your business through new relationships that you overlook those you already have. There's a lot of goodwill to be gained simply by celebrating other people's successes.

I've heard it said that as much as one third of all the content your business pushes through social media could be curated content, produced by someone other than you. I'm not a fan of hard and fast rules but it's absolutely true that you can achieve success simply by passing on material that's of interest to your audience. And if you've taken time to get Point 2 correct then you'll have some clear ideas about what that is.

!GeekAlert - Facebook 'pages to watch'

Facebook makes it easy for you to monitor pages of interest. This could be clients, competitors and any other business on Facebook you want to keep tabs on.

Visit your Facebook Business Page 'Insights' and choose the pages you want to keep an eye on in the 'Pages To Watch' section. You'll be able to see at a glance not just their most recent posts, but their 'top post of the week' – the one with the most engagement, achieving the biggest impact.

This can give you ideas, and inspiration, regarding what works for others, and things to try for yourself. At its simplest, it's a great way to find engaging content to share with your own audience.

Before we wrap this section up and I hand you back to Gary, who is now looking much better on top (either because he is enjoying my brilliant advice or because he's found a bottle of 'Just For Men'), let's have one last look at Point 3 'Give them something they want to share'.

The 'share' bit is essential. In fact, since this is my chapter and I can do what I like...

SHARE.

The idea is you understand your business extremely well, and have a razor sharp understanding of what makes your audience tick, so that when you give them content (a message, a video, a picture etc. etc., whatever it is you 'say' on social media) that content should be so relevant, useful, interesting, helpful, life affirming, entertaining, whatever, that when they receive it, your audience cannot help but pass it on and share it with their own network.

If they do that, they are, in effect, doing your marketing for you. They're taking your message, your brand, your business and forcing it into the news feeds of their friends. When that happens, it's like a snowball rolling down the hill. You're going to gather some serious momentum. You'll build an identity, your follower numbers will increase, people will be drawn to you, you'll be understood, recognised, valued and, best of all, trusted.

Your social media channels should be brimming with content your intended audience can't help but share.

Gillian Reith, from Three Sisters Bake, put it brilliantly when she spoke at our 'Working Digital' conference a few years back: "Every time I'm putting something on our Facebook page, before I hit the 'Post' button, I take a moment to ask myself: If I saw this on someone else's page, would I want to share it? And if the answer is 'No, I wouldn't', then I think very carefully and see if I can improve it, or I'll leave it and say something else."

I'd urge you to consider following Gillian's advice. It ensures a quality threshold and means what you do say will be more effective. There's already plenty of meaningless 'noise' flying around social media. You don't need to add to it. Sometimes just thinking about your message for another 30 seconds or so can give you an idea for a better way to say it, or some fresh inspiration. It can be the difference between content that goes out and just 'sits there' and something that truly connects with people, gains momentum and has an impact.

And that's what we're all striving for: impact.

CHAPTER IN A TWEET

Success on social media comes down to three simple rules:
1. Know your business
2. Know your audience
3. Give them something they want to share

In principle, social media is easy – just give your audience something they'll love. They'll do the marketing for you!

#TrainerLife

Presenting from the cupboard

We've had the pleasure of working in some seriously nice venues. Not just the hi-tech super slick digital enabled conference rooms of the world, but in stately homes, posh hotels, country clubs and more.

It really doesn't take much for a room to be suitable for training. Take the venue we use for our regular Embrace The Space masterclass – we typically hold these in a multi-purpose room that is bright and welcoming, with some suitable tables and chairs and a big screen up front. Add in some wifi, some decent speakers, and a breakout area for lunch and networking and you've got yourself a 'training room'. It's really not difficult.

Despite this, some of the training rooms that we've found ourselves in over the years should have been fined under the Trade Descriptions Act.

Like at the Conference Centre where, when we asked where the projector was, we were directed to the OHP (Overhead Projector) the likes of which I'd not seen in 30 years! Or at the Edinburgh hotel where staff told us that, "No, sorry, there is no wifi, but you should be able to pick up the free wifi from...." actually, I'll let Colin tell you that story later!

The best example though has to be the venue that clearly spent money on getting a fancy projector and speaker system, all built into the wall, with the cables hidden, all out of sight from the attendees. Looked great for sure, but when the main HDMI input at the front of the room failed, it meant no computer access to the projector unless you plugged it in directly, with the laptop needing to sit in the wee cupboard at the back of the room, completely out of sight behind a closed door. Which meant that the presenter ALSO needed to go into the cupboard to use the laptop – something we tend to do a lot of when we're giving live training on Facebook etc.

The result was a number of workshops (because the venue owner didn't really see it as a problem: 'it still works doesn't it?!') where we spent the time going in and out of the cupboard, running back and forth between talking to people from the front of the room, then hiding in the cupboard, using the laptop, shouting through the walls to get the messages across.

The only positive was the fact that the cupboard was also used to store the attendee treats, which included chocolate bars and Haribos. It's surprising how many jelly sweets you can eat while still presenting without the audience even realising it.

Needless to say we stopped using that venue shortly after.

Gary

03

The social platforms explained

(with some help from a teenager)

Gary and Colin tag-team chapter

I've never actually been on a 'whistle-stop' tour and I'm not sure I like the sound of them to be honest. I'd rather take my time, soak up the atmosphere and experience all the sights and sounds.

But that assumes I'm on holiday, perhaps enjoying a city break in somewhere like Barcelona or Florence, with the sun beating down on me and a nice lunch to look forward to.

Twenty-first century social media platforms can't really be compared to popular tourist destinations, so what follows is a 'whistle-stop' tour of some of the most important things you need to know about the main platforms.

This chapter is best enjoyed with your very own whistle, which you can blow at the end of each section. You can purchase a whistle via our affiliate Amazon link here: (https://amzn.to/2YpkExF)[19]

All the stats and information that follows were correct at the time of writing, but the truth is, we cannot keep this type of data up to date in the real world, let alone a book, so don't get too hung up on the numbers we provide, but we hope the 'essence' and explainers should hold true for a while yet!

Following the facts and figures, both Gary and myself give a quick personal summary of what we think of these platforms. As you'll see, contrary to popular belief, we don't always agree!

---

[19] If no whistle link was actually inserted, then a) our proofreader has hugely let us down or b) we decided it was incredibly poor taste to try and make a few pennies from whistle sales on Amazon.

Facebook

Founded in 2004 by Mark Zuckerberg, Facebook is currently the biggest social network of all with over 2.6 billion users (that's well over 30% of the global population!), and arguably the most influential. Predominantly a tool to find and connect with your friends, Facebook's mission is to give people the power  to build communities and bring the world closer together. One of the ways it does this is by gathering huge amounts of data on its users, which is anonymised and made available to advertisers (whose sponsored posts made Facebook a whopping $17.5 billion just in quarter one of 2020 alone).

A growing place for businesses to engage with people, the platform now attracts over 80 million small businesses, providing them with Business Pages to promote and market themselves throughout the Facebook network. Ultimately, Facebook's aim is to convince business owners that they don't need a website, ecommerce system, or mailing list. It can help with all of that, introducing new tools and features on a regular basis, and all for the amazing price of 'free'!

However, as many of them are finding out, thanks to the algorithm, it's now a tougher job to achieve real impact on Facebook than ever before. Love it or hate it, whatever your business, whatever your sector, Facebook's influence on our culture is such that it may be impossible to ignore.

Five Facebook facts (and why they matter):

1. **96% of Facebook users access the platform on their mobile device.**
   If you're using it to drive people to a website (which isn't always the best thing to do), make sure it's a mobile optimised website. Be aware also that the content you post will be seen on a screen approximately 2.5 inches wide, which means that while it looked great when you viewed it on your desktop, the tiny text you were determined to add onto that image is completely illegible. Do more testing of your own page and content on a mobile device!

2. The average business page achieves less than 6% reach on organic posts.

We still come across businesses that don't understand how Facebook works. They think that because they have 1000 people like the page, that 1000 people will see the things they post. The reality is far more challenging. Make sure you understand the algorithm, why it does what it does, and how to improve your chances of doing better than the average.

3. Video posts receive almost four times more engagement than text only.

As we'll repeat many times throughout this book, social media content needs to be visual, and video content is among the best for driving actual audience engagement. No more excuses; do more video will be a common theme in the pages that follow.

4. The average age of a Facebook user is now 40.

Gone are the days when social media was just for the 'young people' (although many business owners still have that mentality). Facebook is now attracting an older audience than ever before, with the 55+ user currently the fastest growing demographic, and the UK average sitting around 40. Young people are still there, though maybe not using it to the same extent or in the same way as they used to. For them it's not really the cool platform it once was (mainly because Granny's now on it), but from a business perspective, the chances are there are more of your customers using it than ever before.

5. Facebook has more features than you probably know about.

As a platform, it's constantly trying to innovate, and add features that extend its usefulness to businesses. From the 'Shop' and 'Services' tabs that enable you to promote (and soon sell) your goods and services respectively, to the 'Notes' tab allowing you to write longer posts (almost blogging), or the 'Jobs' functionality allowing you to post jobs and field applications without ever leaving the platform. It wants to become the only site you need to run your small business online, and while we don't suggest putting all your eggs in Facebook's basket, being aware of what cool tools it has on offer might mean you spot an opportunity to benefit. Head to your page's 'Templates and Tabs' section of the settings, and have a play with the things you're missing.

!GeekAlert

'The Social Network' is a film that claims to tell the story of Facebook's early days. It's a real eye opener and worth a watch if you would like a better understanding of where all this came from.

Another more recent documentary worth a watch is 'The Great Hack' which you'll find on Netflix.

Neither of these films present Facebook in a particularly good light, with the latter especially raising serious issues over how the company uses and exploits your data. So don't blame us if, after watching them, you feel the need to ditch the app, and go live in a lead box 'off grid' up a mountain.

Gary thinks:

With so many people on Facebook it's now impossible to ignore. No matter what your organisation does, having a Facebook business page is, in my opinion, fundamental for operating in today's modern connected world.

Unlike what others often say, I don't think you need to be a B2C[20] business to take advantage of Facebook. Yes, it might favour cafes, consumer brands and sports teams, but I've also seen brilliant results from defence contractors, engineering firms, and big city financial services companies. The aims and objectives for being on Facebook will be different for all companies, but if *people* are important to you (hint – they are, always) then Facebook is the platform to reach them.

So whether it's alerting your customers about the soup of the day, or recruiting your next management trainee, Facebook provides an opportunity for every business. Yes, its reputation has taken a battering recently (as the world finally woke up to how personal data is exploited), and yes, it can be a challenge to achieve 'reach' and impact (given the aggressive algorithm

---

[20] Business to Consumer (as opposed to B2B – Business to Business)

behind it), but to dismiss it on the grounds of not agreeing with the ethics of Mark Zuckerberg, or to turn your back on it due to 'having to resort to Boosting Posts' to see any success, is a misjudged strategy. People are vital to every business, and Facebook has the people. Get over it, and work out a way to benefit.

Colin thinks:

There's still a culture in some businesses which think they're a bit 'above' social media, too serious, too important, too clever or 'we don't deal with the public', and I actually find that attitude a little arrogant. Bearing in mind the number of people using Facebook and the geographical and demographical spread of them, can you really afford to turn them off and not engage with them? It's the communication method of choice for a huge chunk of the world's population and you probably should be there. Not to speak to EVERYONE and maybe not even to promote every aspect of your business. But if you can't find any use at all for it, I'd suggest there are some pretty deep problems in your business.

Instagram

Owned by Facebook, the second biggest social network on the planet[21] commands a huge audience share in its own right, with over 1.1 billion monthly active users, many of them much younger than those regularly frequenting the parent company platform (with the average user aged just 22).

Arguably a much simpler offering than Facebook, Instagram involves the posting of images or videos, alongside a text description (or caption), sharing it to your followers while hoping a wider audience (who don't yet know you) find you through clever use of hashtags or geolocation.

Over a decade since its inception, Instagram has evolved beyond the typical curated feed of perfect photos (where image filters ensure Gary's frown lines remain hidden from public view), with newer features such as 'Stories' and 'IG TV' becoming core to its future success.

With over 90% of users happy to follow at least one business on Instagram, brands large and small are flocking to it, eager to reach younger audiences, through a mix of organic and paid for content (the latter being controlled through Facebook's powerful advertising systems).

Interesting Instagram Insights:

1. **Hashtags help achieve a bigger reach (and engagement).**
   Hashtags are a common feature on Instagram, and every post can have up to 30 of them added to the image or video caption. Unless you're a big name celebrity and everybody already knows you, hashtags help you get found by others, while also aiming to increase engagement on the post itself.

2. **Instagram Stories are now more popular than the main feed.**
   Recent stats from Instagram suggest that the 'stories' feature on the

---

[21] This is debatable, and depends on whether you consider YouTube, WhatsApp or WeChat social networks.

platform now attracts more daily users than the traditional curated feed. Originally 'borrowed' from Snapchat, stories on Instagram now see over half a billion people daily swiping through 'throw-away' content from their friends, celebrities, and business brands.

3. **Instagram attracts more Social Influencers than any other platform.**
A growing trend in marketing, more and more businesses are utilising influencers to help them sell more products, or gain increased market share. Instagram is arguably the home of influencer marketing, with beauty, travel, and sporting brands being most likely to consider this a viable route to market. If this appeals to you, make sure you read Chapter 11 before you jump in and identify that 'on trend' reality TV star with three million followers just waiting to hear about your new pore minimiser cream.

!GeekAlert - the # explained

'Hashtags' were popularised by Twitter but are now used extensively across Instagram, and to a lesser extent on Facebook and LinkedIn. Using hashtags can increase the reach of your posts, as it allows new people to find you based on you sharing content that's relevant to them.

Instagram now allows people to follow hashtags directly, and you can see this data from their profile. So if you wanted to get a post in front of @richardbranson (who might never choose to follow you) then a quick check shows that what he does follow (among others) is the hashtag #virginfamily. If your next post contains that same hashtag, then bingo – Richard's just seen it[22].

No one owns or controls them and just because you can add up to 30 on a single Instagram post doesn't mean you always should. The trick is to think about what hashtags people who haven't heard of your business might be using. So hashtags relating to a geographical location e.g. #glasgow, or a discipline #customerservice, or something you're pretty confident people

---

[22] Please use this tactic both strategically, and respectfully. Don't just go spamming Richard Branson on Instagram (or anyone else for that matter) and only use hashtags which are truly relevant to your post.

would find relevant to your post, such as #cutedogs #ITJobs. Don't be spammy or abuse hashtags and don't use them as a form of punctuation like teenagers do: #bored #whenslunch #storming. These all work, in that you can click on them and see a stream of content all under that same hashtag, but there's little return in it for your business.

Check out these sites to give you some creative hashtag ideas, while avoiding any that are blacklisted:
https://bit.ly/etsbook-allhashtag
https://bit.ly/etsbook-bannedhashtags[23]

Gary thinks:

Instagram is one of the cool tools to play with right now. It's no longer just bodybuilders, models, entrepreneurs and other influencers[24] that are seeing the benefits but businesses of all shapes and sizes. If you can bring your business to life in images and video (and if you can't, you have bigger issues), then you can get a result from Instagram. Yes, it might attract a younger audience (which is getting older on a daily basis) and be better suited to a florist, or fashion designer, but I've seen some brilliant Insta-results from financial firms, local councils, charities and more. The human brain is a 'visual thing' – we like looking at pretty pictures and videos. Use Instagram to inspire people, and to showcase (visually) all aspects of what you do.

Some of our own best posts on Instagram highlight the locations we visit for training, and the people on our courses, but don't think you need to post flawless photos to get a result. Take a look at the World Health Organisation[25] and see how they use it for amazing infographics, and the presentation of statistics etc. Or take a look at the global power giant, General Electric, and you'll see their primary Instagram strategy is to highlight company culture and champion their diverse workforce.

---

[23] Warning: as you can probably guess - many naughty words get banned on Instagram!
[24] Note that being a bodybuilder, model or entrepreneur does not immediately make you an influencer.
[25] Who? Sorry, I can't help myself saying that in workshops; you'll have to suffer bad jokes here too.

Top tip: don't expect Instagram to drive much traffic to your website. It'll rank as one of the worst social platforms for referring web traffic if that's all you're trying to do with it. Instead have some fun; post selfies, use hashtags, play with Instagram Stories, or create short videos in 'Reels' - their latest feature which aims to take on TikTok with augmented reality filters, timers and music options. You might even enjoy it! It's the second biggest social networking platform (owned by the first biggest) and it's not going away anytime soon.

Colin thinks:

I'm still not a huge Instagram fan. I was late getting onto it and feel my business doesn't find it as easy to create visuals as others. If I was selling physical products, or designing cakes or dresses, or had a beautiful view out my window, it would be easier I think. I think businesses are judged more harshly on Instagram if it doesn't look right. If your feed of images looks out of date, or messy or just doesn't do you justice, I think it can be a real turn off.

All that said, just look at the numbers, as Gary outlines above. The opportunity for huge reach is incredible. You don't need to be doing anything sensational either; a bit of effort goes a long way. And while I haven't quite found my feet with functions like Instagram Stories and live videos on Instagram, I know other business owners who have and they are getting amazing results. I think if you got into social media a bit earlier, like I did, and favoured Twitter first, you might always feel a bit resistant to Instagram. But if you got started later, or if you are starting now, I'd say absolutely prioritise Instagram, certainly over Twitter, maybe even more than Facebook because of the opportunities for increased reach and engagement.

Twitter

One of the original pillars of social media, Twitter's popularity grew dramatically in the early days thanks to celebrity and political endorsements. Lately however, as a business, Twitter hasn't been doing so well. It has slipped from being the second most popular social network to a distant third, fourth or fifth (depending on how you measure it).

That said, there's still a significant volume of people using it, and it remains extremely popular as a news gathering channel. A great many journalists are active on it and use it to share news and information and to connect with potential sources.

Top Twitter Tuition[26]:

1. Consistent user numbers but decreasing engagement.

With approximately 330 million monthly active users, Twitter's numbers have remained stable over the past few years, and while that figure sounds small compared to Facebook (it's approx. an eighth of their user base) it's still a huge number. What has decreased, however, is engagement. The 'back and forth' chat and discussion which Twitter was renowned for in years gone by has faded, with more people now admitting to using it in a passive manner, rather than contributing to the conversation. Just because they're not engaging, doesn't mean they're not seeing it, so check your data, and aim to increase your reach.

2. Twitter is still the most popular customer service channel.

Despite lower user numbers, Twitter's actual usage as a customer service channel is among the highest (if not sitting at the top). Our own Social Media and Customer Service workshops regularly prove that consumers head to Twitter when they want something sorted, and most expect a response within the hour. How do you measure up?

---

[26] My attempts at alliteration for these headings are beginning to wane.

3. Anti-Social behaviour still a problem.

It's easy to be anonymous on Twitter and unfortunately it still attracts a significant volume of anti-social behaviour, with bullying and harassment not uncommon. While we'll assume that you're not in the habit of displaying such behaviours, don't forget any staff or freelancers you use who (by association) represent your brand. Make sure you've got a suitable social media policy in place, and head over to Chapter 13 for more advice on protecting your reputation from poorly judged activity.

4. A focus on 'what's happening now' and breaking news.

Twitter is still a popular destination for anything considered 'breaking news' with its mainly chronological feed lending itself to people knowing what's current and trending. The topic of 'news' was the most cited reason that people use it. Most businesses have a need to communicate an aspect of 'real time' with their customers (such as late availability, flash sales, or cancellations) and Twitter could be the place to exploit it. For an extreme example of this, check out our Albions Oven story in the nostalgic classic case studies later on.

!GeekAlert - Twitter lists

One of the most beneficial features of Twitter (yet often the most under-utilised) is the ability to organise the accounts you follow into lists.

We're often told that the biggest negative about Twitter is 'information overload'. This gets worse the more people/brands/celebrities and news organisations you follow, and because some people take the 'What's happening?' prompt literally, it can often mean your feed is jam packed with tweets, not all of them oozing value.

You can begin to solve this issue by grouping accounts together into specific Twitter lists. How you configure these is up to you, but we'd suggest a list for your industry influencers, one for your competitors (allowing you to see what they're busy talking about), maybe one for your staff, and a separate one for your personal friends and family. You could take things further and create dynamic lists of current customers, or lists of prospective new clients.

Now you can choose what you want to see, rather than be shown the default 'one huge stream of noise'. It allows more strategic use of the platform, and ensures you don't miss the important tweets.

Lists can be public (where anyone can find, see and follow the lists you've created), or private (purely for your own usage) and no, the people you've added do NOT get alerted!

Up your Twitter game and set up some Lists.

Gary thinks:

Twitter might have fallen from grace over the last few years, and certainly when you compare the numbers and the growth (or lack of it) to the likes of Facebook or Instagram it might look like a platform in trouble. In truth it's still got a huge volume of people on it, who still get a lot of value from it, and who are often very loyal to it. It's where many people still get the bulk of their news; Twitter, in my opinion, is still a superb platform for #breakingnews, and I don't just mean #brexit or #covid19, I mean real-time relevant news from my kid's primary school, or the latest score from the football game I care about, or last minute availability for the workshop I want to attend.

It should be treated differently to how you use Facebook and other platforms, and as a business you should consider Twitter for delivering better customer service (more on that later), to share great links and articles, to answer your customers' questions, and to get a better understanding of the 'word on the street'. Use Twitter like a search engine, to 'listen' to what people are saying. Your customers, your industry, your local area. Find your own business opportunities by engaging with people moaning about your competitors (be careful how you do it!), and make sure your 'Bio' is a good one, helping explain to anyone who you are, what you do, and why they should care about you.

Colin thinks:

Were it not for Twitter, Gary and I might never have worked together. And there are several other important business and personal relationships I enjoy today which just wouldn't be the same without it. It was the first social network I joined and used properly (although I'd played around with Bebo and MySpace) and I remember using it without a web browser or app and everything went through your mobile phone like an SMS text message. It didn't even support adding a picture to your Tweets in those days.

The journalist in me loves it too because of its emphasis on breaking news or 'what's happening now'. I think it's revolutionised news gathering and our relationship with the mass media. It's made the world a more equal place, exposed corrupt regimes and made it easier for whistleblowers to put sensitive information in the public domain. In my days as a radio presenter it gave me a direct route to my audience, and them to me, in a way that I could never have imagined a few years earlier.

These days, there's way too much nasty, divisive political discussion for my liking and some people I know experience regular, horrendous abuse, sexism and misogyny when they use it. That said, having already built a community based around the topics I'm interested in and the people I like, when I log on, I am shielded from the worst of it.

If I was starting now and was only concerned with promoting my business, I wouldn't use Twitter and would put all my energies into Instagram. But that's not my approach at all. I use social media platforms because I like them, I see a result from them, and to this day, Twitter remains my favourite.

!GeekAlert - Colin's clever Twitter #hashtag hack

I've had success with hashtags by relating them to popular TV programmes. Remember, golden rule two: 'Know the audience' (which includes understanding what they watch on TV, which radio station they listen to, and what shops they visit on the high street).

So if my audience is small business owners who watch Dragon's Den on a Sunday evening, I might Tweet some opinions on the business owners who are pitching and share some advice I would give them if they came to my presentation skills training course.

I could add #BBCDragonsDen at the end and this might now be seen by people who don't know me and don't follow me, but who happen to be watching the same TV programme and following that same hashtag. My hope would be that they then see me, follow me, read some of my other tweets, decide maybe I know a thing or two about all this, visit my website and enquire as to how I might help them. And it absolutely has been the result, several times, exactly as I've outlined here, and led to work.

YouTube

YouTube is a video sharing platform, owned by Google, and holds the title of being the second largest search engine in the world. Who wouldn't want a presence on it?!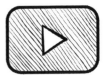

The internet as a whole has become much more focussed around videos in the last decade or so and YouTube has been at the absolute heart of that growth since its launch in 2006. By uploading content to YouTube you can give your business a significant boost on Google's own search engine; it will often return video results, from YouTube, in the main 'Page 1' Google results for particular search terms. If search engine optimisation (SEO) is an important part of your business marketing strategy, then a YouTube presence can really help.

Over and above that, we are increasingly seeing audiences, when they're looking for information or advice, moving away from the standard Google Search and simply opening the YouTube app on their smartphones. You'll have heard the phrase 'show, don't tell', well, many people perceive websites as bland, biased destinations where you'll tell me (because you're biased) how wonderful your business is. And I don't get to see what it's *really* like. Whereas the same search on YouTube might provide more interesting results. Videos, with perhaps a real human being in them, offering a chance to get to know you in a more authentic way, and maybe some behind-the-scenes clips. Video is much more engaging than words on a website, and YouTube is seen as a more exciting platform than a search engine which delivers little more than a list of pages.

All this is driven by technology. The early days of the internet meant dial up modems, and pre-iPhone and pre-3G mobile phones, we simply couldn't consume video in a convenient way. That's all changed now and whether it's instructional videos, virtual tours, behind-the-scenes fun or something else, video should be a big part of your social media use. You might get more engagement by putting your videos on Instagram, Facebook and LinkedIn, but to ensure a longer shelf life and to get the search engine benefits we've mentioned, make sure you put them on YouTube too.

YouTube User Guide

1. Like all the others, YouTube has an algorithm.

Give your videos a better chance of being seen by choosing the title of each one very carefully. In the same way as the text on your website is carefully considered to relate to keywords potential customers might use, you should do the same with content you put on YouTube. Fill out the title, description and add relevant tags.

2. Be prepared to take part.

YouTube is more than a video hosting or video sharing platform. It's a community. People can subscribe to your channel (which means they're much more likely to see each video you publish), they can comment on your videos and 'like' them too. Raise your profile by doing the same with others. Those who enjoy the most success contribute *to* the platform, as well as using it for themselves. Be there because you enjoy being there and interacting, rather than seeing it simply as a marketing activity.

3. Length matters.

My favourite question is: 'How long should my video be?'. A nice answer, which my friend James Cridland uses when he's asked the same about podcasts, is 'as long as it needs to be but not a second longer'. That's a good rule of thumb. There's no easy answer and you should know, from your own analytics and data, whether your shorter videos perform better, or whether your audience will keep watching for 10, 20, even 30 minutes. So vary it and try things out, but in general, a good tip is to consider cutting videos into 'bite size' chunks. In my experience, a series of four five-minute videos tends to achieve a better result than a single 20 minute video.

YouTube's algorithm comes into play here too. It penalises your video (and sends it further down the search result rankings) if people don't watch all the way to the end. If people do, it's a gold star for you and you'll climb the results and get even more viewers. Another important point to consider is to what extent does your video contribute to viewers spending more time on YouTube. So make use of 'cards' and 'end screens' and the other elements where your videos can include links to other YouTube videos. People might get bored with your content but if they go from your video to something else that keeps them on YouTube, then it'll be your video that gets the credit. You should also consider curating your own, and other people's video content into playlists.

Gary thinks:

I worry about any business that doesn't have any sort of 'video strategy' right now. Video content is HOT, so if you're not making any, you're missing out. YouTube is the go-to place for video, and it's owned by Google, meaning it gets a favourable listing in the search results so long as you understand the basics of SEO (see our bonus chapter near the end of the book). My kids come home from school and turn on YouTube in the same way that I used to (in the olden days[27]) come home and turn on the telly. The truth is, they don't even wait until they're home; they watch the latest stupid viral video on their mobile phones while walking home. It's not just kids and silly videos. It's everyone, and the numbers don't lie. If YouTube is just the 'new telly', then we can all now afford to create content for people to consume (in ways we never could in the olden days). Fun videos, educational videos, how-to content, behind-the-scenes of my business content, and yes, even cat videos. Estimates (from people who know more than us!) are that in the next couple of years well over 80% of all internet traffic will be video. YouTube and Google will continue to be a major player in this space. Get yourself a YouTube channel, and start making videos!!!

Colin thinks:

Making videos and uploading them to YouTube is one thing, but getting them seen, is another. Just as there's an art to getting the ranking you want on Google, think carefully about the titles you use for YouTube videos. Be sure to fill out the description, add tags, generate captions and use a tool like Canva.com to design a good looking thumbnail.

Spend time thinking about the videos you could create. Specific, tutorial based content, based on what people are searching for such as 'How To Use The Yoast PlugIn To Change The Title Of Your Website' will likely get far more views than something vague and generic like 'More SEO tips'.

---

[27] My kids refer to anything before 2010 as the 'olden days', and they genuinely feel sorry for me that we only had four TV channels, and had to wait 28 days delivery as standard.

I believe there's a generation coming up who won't use Google the way some of us older members of society do. For us, a tool like Google replaced the likes of the Yellow Pages. It's a list. A directory. Younger people growing up in a world AFTER the demise of the Yellow Pages won't need something to replace it. They see the entire internet as an entertainment platform, rather than an information platform. The risk is, when they need the services of a plumber, for example, they never even 'look' for a plumber, they just engage the services of the plumber that's been making them laugh on YouTube for the last few years. Or they try and fix the fault themselves and engage with the company that's posted some videos giving instructions on how to do these basic jobs. To a section of society, the risk is, if you're not on YouTube, you become invisible.

!GeekAlert

YouTube has its own built-in video editor but it's quite basic and the music they make available to put on videos is quite limited. You'll find wider selections at sites such as BenSound.com, PremiumBeat.com and many others.

For video editing we recommend LumaFusion and Quik, and for more control of your smartphone camera, check out Filmic Pro.

LinkedIn

With over 500 million users across 200 countries, LinkedIn is considered the world's largest professional network. Since 2015 it's been owned by Microsoft, and surprisingly for some, their purchase of it didn't ruin it, but arguably made it bigger and better.

Filled with a wide mix of 'professional people' (the majority being in their early thirties), the users of LinkedIn are an active bunch, with well over half of them checking it daily, accessing it from both mobile phones and desktop devices. LinkedIn had to be included in a book about business usage of social media as it's a place where actual business happens (unlike most of the other platforms, where cat videos reign supreme).

Lovely LinkedIn Learnings[28]

1. Try (but don't buy) Premium.

LinkedIn will regularly tempt you into upgrading your account, encouraging you to buy a 'premium' subscription promising many benefits as a result. For most small business owners there's no real value, and all you'll end up is £40 a month worse off. Being a premium user won't suddenly make LinkedIn work for you. It's not a shortcut to success, and instead we advocate that everyone should simply understand how to get more from the platform without paying, and only then (once you're already killing it) maybe consider further upping your game by exploring premium. They usually offer a trial period, so feel free to road-test it, but think carefully about whether it's really worth it.

2. Personal profiles over company pages.

Many people ask us: 'How do I create a business page on LinkedIn?'. And they're right to ask: you certainly should create one, but understand that it might not deliver much value for you. LinkedIn is a people-to-people network. People go there to connect with individuals with various skills,

---

[28] Taking it too far now.....

or who inspire them, or share great content. Yes, have a business page, but more importantly, be there yourself, with a personal, fully completed professional profile. And encourage all your staff to do the same too! It's YOU that someone will connect with, and YOU that can proactively connect with others. The business page is nice to have, but for most it's quite a passive thing, sitting there waiting for people to visit, most of whom do so because they're looking to find the right person in your company to connect with!

3. Don't just be there.....actually use it!

We know from experience that many people are *on* LinkedIn, but are often not actually using it. They've got a profile, set up years ago, but haven't connected to anyone in a while (probably ignoring the last dozen requests from others, with a 'why do they want to connect with me' attitude). And as for saying anything, it has maybe been years since your last post, if you've even said anything at all! If this all sounds familiar, then you need to change. LinkedIn rewards the people who use it. It features your content higher in their algorithm, it ranks your profile higher in the results, it suggests you as a possible connection request to other relevant people more if you're an actual active user. Share content, post industry news, connect with others, add more skills, ask for more recommendations. It's no coincidence that the people who are there, but don't use LinkedIn, are the same people who admit to not really seeing any benefit from it. The ones who actively use it, keep actively using it for a reason – because it works!

Colin thinks:

It's taken a long time, but now, some 11 years after I joined, LinkedIn is by far the most useful social network for my business. For a while, I was there, with a profile and very little happened, but now I can post an update, receive engagement and I know, beyond any doubt, that LinkedIn delivers value to my business. Engagement, connections, leads, customers and hard cash..... it's definitely driving value.

What's the secret? An element of perseverance (posting things continually even when little engagement was coming back), and contributing *to* the platform (commenting on others and sharing their posts) rather than only being concerned with what I was saying about myself.

The real results started coming when I had a clear idea of who my audience was. I remember vividly the moment I finally realised I'd worked out what my business does and who it was for. That was a game changer. I can walk down the street and pretty much pick out my potential customers. I understand their problems and what I can offer to help them. And all of that, informs my content, the things I say on LinkedIn, and that, in turn, gets results.

Gary thinks:

LinkedIn is often referred to as the dull, boring, corporate platform, used by dull boring people in suits. Usually people calling it that haven't logged on in a long time. LinkedIn has massively improved over the last few years, and now attracts a much wider audience than ever before.

Essentially, LinkedIn is 'Facebook with its Tie on'[29]. It's an almost identical platform technically, the main difference being the content that flows through it. Business content. Not just dull boring corporate business content, but exciting, entrepreneurial, dynamic updates from anyone in business. LinkedIn is no longer just the home of lawyers, accountants and estate agents[30], but the social platform of choice for anyone in business who wants to connect with people. From sole trader plumbers, to professional footballers, from start-up dog-walkers, to CEOs of large city financial firms.

LinkedIn is very much a pro-active tool (don't expect much to happen just by 'being there'). To get the most from it, you need to know who you want to connect with. Ask yourself the question: 'Who, if they knew about me, would mean a possible business opportunity?'. If you're a web designer, and you've just done some amazing web design work for a well-known restaurant, wouldn't you like other restaurant owners to know about you (and the amazing work you do in their sector). If you've noticed more work recently from your local council, wouldn't you like to connect with more decision makers in that same organisation, as well as nudge other local council officials to be aware of you and your work?

---

[29] In our workshops I always say that while miming putting on a tie. Colin is well versed at laughing on cue when I do this, but the truth is he's seen it 186 times and smiles out of sympathy.
[30] No offence to lawyers, accountants and estate agents.

Business has always been about 'who you know' (arguably just as much as it is about what you do). LinkedIn is a people connecting tool. It's a damn good one, and the opportunities, once you connect with the right people, usually end up presenting themselves at some point.

!GeekAlert - The power of LinkedIn search filters

One of our favourite demos to show at our workshops is how powerful LinkedIn search can be. Most users of the platform only scratch the surface of it, using it to try and find a few specific people by their name. But by utilising the advanced search filters, it's amazing who you can find and connect with.

As an example let's say you're starting up a small fashion brand, making cashmere scarves from your back bedroom. You want the right people to know about your awesome product, and you want to sell more of it.

You could speak to a business adviser and ask them to help you research the fashion retail industry. Or you could buy a list from a (*cough*) reputable 'email list company' and email[31] everyone, asking if they'd like to meet you for coffee. Or you could Google 'fashion retailers', visit 50 relevant websites, find the published telephone number, call them and ask to speak to their fashion buyers. Good luck with that.

There's lots of things you could do.

You could also turn to LinkedIn and search for the phrase 'buyer'. It will return around two million people who are indeed buyers. If you stop there (as most people do) it won't do very much for you. Good luck talking to two million buyers today, from every industry and location. Instead click on 'Filters', and change your location to 'Glasgow', change industry to 'Apparel and Fashion', and hit apply. Now you've got approximately 50 people looking back at you. Fashion buyers from retailers such as Quiz clothing, H&M, TopShop, Gautier,

---

[31] By email, we mean spam.

Next, and many more. Now you have a manageable 'hit list' which you can work your way through and make some meaningful personalised connection requests, connecting with key players in the industry you want to break into.

If you're a supplier who sells to local authorities, go and search for 'procurement' people within every council (you can filter by 'current company'). If you specialise in software for schools, go and find everyone in the 'Education' sector, using the keyword 'IT'. If you specialise in Drone video footage, seek out everyone on LinkedIn (in your area) who offers 'Photography' as a service (another filter) and suggest some collaboration.

LinkedIn is the new Yellow Pages on steroids. Work out who you want to connect with, and proactively go and find them.

#business   #banter

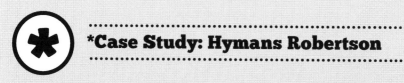

*Case Study: Hymans Robertson

Financial services firm Hymans Robertson make a great case study in their approach to strategic use of social media, specifically in the way they have embraced LinkedIn to develop staff opportunities and to grow the business as a whole.

Rather than just keeping social within the 'marketing' box (as so many bigger businesses do), Hymans realised that much of their business (pensions and investments advice and consultancy) came from their employees' client relationships. They recognised that individual usage of social media could enhance and increase that personal, trusted advisor approach that worked so well for them.

While not mandatory, all staff, regardless of role or seniority, are strongly encouraged to attend a day's social media training, where both the opportunities and pitfalls are explained in detail, with a focus given to LinkedIn and how it can be used to nurture existing client relationships, but also to find and develop new ones.

Approximately 25% (and growing) of their 1,000 employees across their four UK offices, now use LinkedIn as part of their regular day to day activities, sharing news, financial advice, making new connections, and learning from their peers. The official Hyman's company page on LinkedIn has over 7000 followers, which sounds impressive, but when you consider the combined reach of the staff (estimated at approx. half a million) you realise the 'power of the people' to make an impact.

For those staff who aren't quite confident enough to share their own experience and 'thought leadership' on LinkedIn, they can take advantage of a weekly 'social news' internal newsletter, highlighting worthy sharable content, and providing a nudge on relevant trending topics.

Commenting on the value of LinkedIn to the organisation, head of Coaching and Development, Monica Smith had this to say:

"LinkedIn is a natural fit to help our staff build relationships, and to convey what we do as a company through our people. Staff who might have found it difficult to lift the phone, have used LinkedIn to build strong, valuable networks by connecting with and following industry leaders. Most of the team are now confidently creating and sharing interesting content, increasing their own reputations, and that of the company as a whole."

While far from encouraging a 'free for all', Hymans encourages staff to be themselves, whilst providing light touch guidelines on boundaries that maintain professionalism. Their simple to read, easy to understand social media guidelines and policy document is firmly rooted in the following introductory statement:

"No matter who your message is aimed at, remember to help, inform or engage, and never discriminate or offend. Overall, it's just about common sense." Good advice for any business.

Pinterest

Pinterest doesn't consider itself a social network, instead defining the platform as a 'Catalogue of Ideas'. While we agree with the sentiment, we also respectfully disagree that it's not a social platform. With over 335 million monthly active users (and still growing fast!), Pinterest's ability to influence people into taking action is perhaps what sets it apart from all the other platforms put together.

At its core, Pinterest is a 'scrap book' (or a series of 'mood boards' for the designers out there), allowing people to pin things that interest them, and return to them later. But that 'visual bookmark' doesn't just exist for them; it can be seen by friends, family, peers, or indeed anyone on the whole platform. With 50% of users claiming to have made a purchase based on something seen on Pinterest, it's a valuable platform that many more businesses should be taking advantage of.

Persuasive Pinterest Pointers[32]

1. It's maybe already driving traffic to you.

Years ago we had a client who asked us to audit where all their web traffic was coming from. A quick dig into Google Analytics and we discovered that 38% of referring traffic was coming from Pinterest. When we told the client this, their response was: 'What on earth is Pinterest?'. Our reply: 'If you knew, it would be driving even more traffic to you'. People are likely already pinning your images, especially if your website contains lots of amazing inspiring pictures (the client in question was a small B&B in the Scottish highlands, and their website contained beautiful images of the Scottish countryside). But by actually having a business Pinterest page yourself, and actively pinning up your own images, you'll see an even bigger impact, with increased levels of activity.

---

[32] Seriously, that sounds like a breed of dog.

2. It's all about the 'click'.

People use Pinterest to find things. Everything from new shoes, fridge freezers, holiday destinations, tofu recipes, training workshops, 50th birthday cakes and more. It's a research tool, and customers start every journey by researching possibilities. Once they find you, you need to ensure they can 'click' for more. Click to your website where they can buy the shoes. Click to your YouTube channel where they can watch even more videos. Click through to your Facebook Messenger where they can order the cake. Pinterest will often be one of your best referrers of traffic, so long as you're adding pins which contain a hyperlink back to your destination of choice.

3. Pinterest and Google play nice together.

Unlike other social platforms, Google still likes Pinterest. It pretty much hates Facebook (grudgingly adding Facebook links to its listings), and its relationship with Twitter over the years has been chequered to say the least. Consider Pinterest an extension of your search engine efforts. Knowing that your pins won't just be found on Pinterest directly, but via Google too. Remember to follow SEO best practices (see our bonus chapter at the end) and consider the words used in your Pin titles and descriptions. Specifically remember that Pinterest is a tool where people search for very specific things; so make sure the title of your Pin is 'Lilac blue kitten heel shoes perfect for a wedding' and not just 'shoes'.

4. The perfect partner for Ecommerce.

If you're selling online then Pinterest should be well established in your bag of tricks. Ensuring you've 'claimed' your website is just the start, following which you could look at 'Rich Pins' of products which pull in dynamic pricing, stock availability and more. Some ecommerce platforms easily integrate with Pinterest allowing you to automate everything, grabbing your pictures, descriptions and other data, adding them to your relevant pin boards, and giving you the option of additional advertising on top. Online traders in the states have been switched onto Pinterest for years, and here in the UK we need to catch up quick!

Colin thinks:

If Twitter is the most labour intensive of all the major social platforms (you have to say A LOT to have any hope of breaking through the noise and building an audience, and Tweets have a very short shelf life) then Pinterest is surely the least labour intensive. You can upload images to Pinterest today, fill out the description on each one with a link to your website, and enjoy the resulting traffic for months and years to come, without doing ANYTHING! That alone makes it worth considering. There's little chat and not much engagement. If you don't enjoy writing this could be the place for you! And with clever tools such as the PinIt browser button, Tailwind or Hootsuite, there's very little extra work involved in taking images from your website or other social channels and adding them here too. Pinterest is also largely free from the 'nasty' elements that can be found on other social networks.

Gary thinks:

NSDesign is NOT a typical Pinterest business. We're not in the wedding or fashion industry. We don't produce cooking recipes or ideas to help you redesign your living room. And we don't help you with suggestions of creative activities for the whole family during lockdown!

That said, our Pinterest page gets over 2000 monthly unique views for almost zero effort. 2000 people a month 'see us' through our images (and occasional videos) added to Pinterest automatically without any human effort whatsoever (see the #GeekAlert at the end of this chapter for how we do this). Many of these pins link back to our website, our blog posts, or training services. Many link to Instagram or other social platforms, and many are simply 're-pins' from other people, usually cool social media infographics or funny memes. Not all of our 2000 views result in clicks, but for almost zero effort, for a 'non-typical' Pinterest business, we do alright!

Now consider the impact for businesses which are more suited to the platform. The businesses which are producing content regularly that people do try and find, and pin to their boards. Pinterest is a valuable research platform for the users looking to find ideas and inspiration, increase creativity, find things to do or make, discover new hobbies, share cool stuff and find things to buy. Pinterest and ecommerce are a no-brainer, with 'discovery shopping' a growing trend in how people now find and buy anything and everything. No matter who you are, or what industry you're in, as Colin says above, given Pinterest is possibly the least labour intensive platform to actually get results from, you've no excuse not to give it a try, and see (even a small increase) in website referral traffic, and people discovering your organisation.

!GeekAlert

Add the PinIt button to your web browser of choice, and you'll be able to add images you find across the internet to Pinterest at the touch of a button. Makes adding your own website images, and others from across the web, much easier and increases the chances of you maintaining active boards with regular new pins. Just remember to go back and 'edit' the pins and tailor the titles and descriptions.

https://bit.ly/etsbook-pinterestbutton

*Case Study: The Little Art School

Art is a skill which can be taught. That's the belief of Little Art School founder Joanne Robinson, who passionately encourages kids of all ages to attend drawing and painting courses where they learn not just the artistic skills and techniques you'd expect, but more importantly, self-esteem.

With plans for a UK wide franchise model moving along at pace, the COVID-19 lockdown forced the Little Art School team to identify temporary alternative delivery methods over the typical classroom teaching format.

They turned to Pinterest. A channel they'd had setup for years, but hardly touched. Whether a stroke of luck, or a stroke of genius, this move turned out to be a resounding business success on so many levels.

Joanne explained: "When lockdown hit we knew that we couldn't run any of our studio-based classes, which was ironic because one of the things we could hear from everyone was an even bigger desire from parents to keep their children busy, entertained, and if possible educated during these challenging times. Home schooling for so many has involved finding videos for the kids to watch on YouTube, and searching Pinterest for creative activities to keep them stimulated. Despite our concerns, we knew that there was an opportunity here for our digital channels.

"We decided to take our teaching online through the lockdown, so that our students could continue to draw and paint, and through a series of YouTube videos, we launched a new 'Daily Draw' initiative, where we teach viewers to draw (or paint) something recognisable and familiar to them – from Darth Vader and Yoda, to Super Mario and Spiderman, fun characters and objects that kids would want to know how to draw better.

"The concept proved a success beyond anything we could have imagined. What we had designed for our artists was being picked up by families right across the UK and in fact across the world. However, we felt we could extend that reach and we decided to start using Pinterest to promote things. Pinterest is the perfect 'find things to do' channel, and the users fit our target demographic perfectly – parents (particularly mums) of young kids. It was perfect for us and we knew it, but until this time hadn't really given it any investment in time or effort. Four months and approx. 500 pins later, and Pinterest is firmly established in our digital strategy. We have been absolutely blown away by the new reach Pinterest has opened up to us.

"Posting (sorry - Pinning!) a mix of artistic tips and techniques, artists we love, books we recommend, galleries we hope (soon) to visit, and of course our daily draw challenges, from almost nothing our channel is now achieving over 35,000 monthly views, a number that is climbing so rapidly we can't keep up! Many of them are turning into clicks to our YouTube channel, as well as our website and other social platforms. All at zero cost. It wasn't the case a few months ago, but I genuinely now love Pinterest and can demonstrate a significant return on the minimal investment (just my time!) and wider marketing benefits for the company.

"Even when things start getting back to normal, we'll continue to prioritise Pinterest as a key channel to reach, help and excite our customers. I'm even tempted to start looking at paid activity too! My only regret is not starting to regularly Pin sooner. This isn't just an additional marketing channel for us, I can see it becoming the keystone of how we grow our brand to reach new markets."

Snapchat

As Facebook became a behemoth, with everyone and their Grandmother opening an account, and businesses jumping all over it to promote and sell things, what was the discerning teenager supposed to do? Many wanted to start again, with a space they could call their own, that their parents wouldn't be able to understand. Even better  if the messages they sent each other could be made to 'disappear' after 30 seconds. Haha! No more 'social media faux pas' coming up in search results and screwing up their employment prospects.

With that and some big name celebrity endorsements, Snapchat was on its way.

And its growth was pretty phenomenal until Instagram and TikTok developed their own platforms to include many of the elements Snapchat made popular in the first place.

We see Snapchat more as a multi-media messaging platform than a social network. You can't search for 'plumber Glasgow' and find Glasgow plumbers. You'd need to know their user name or scan their Snapchat code. It's almost impossible for a business to 'find' individual users and follow them, like they could on Twitter.

Serious Snapchat Stats

1. **It's not as 'transient' as was originally made out.**
   That stuff about messages 'disappearing' 30 seconds after they are received? It's not quite that simple, as Snapchat keeps everything on its servers and has, on some occasions, handed it over to the authorities when asked to. We know of several cases (even in our local areas) where young people shared particular images they went on to bitterly regret.

2. **Snapchat dabbles in Wearable Tech.**
   Snapchat Spectacles are best described as expensive, garish, chunky

sunglasses with a button on the frame that records 30 second bursts of video and posts them to Snapchat. Colin couldn't resist and forked out £150 to be among the first to own a pair and then realised they look ridiculous. Plus he doesn't do anything interesting enough to merit filming. But perhaps you do, and the principle of wearable tech – glasses that record whatever you're looking at – probably will have some impact on the way we do things. It opens up some interesting new angles for video, such as the view from the Chef's eyeline as they chop up veg to prepare a meal. Or a mountain biker tearing down a hillside. Snapchat didn't get it right in the versions we've seen so far but it's worth keeping an eye (or two!) on this.

3. **It has a lexicon all of its own.**

Slang, acronyms, emojis, a rainbow coming out your tongue and cat ears EVERYWHERE. To get anywhere on Snapchat you need to embrace a very different form of communication. Some big brands and celebrities do it well and have been able to develop a following and grow their businesses, but many end up wasting their time or making fools of themselves.

Colin thinks:

I think Snapchat is stuck. Instagram copied it, then TikTok improved upon it. It's sitting there, with a passionate user base but not much growth and most of the businesses that I deal with, don't bother with it. It's barely a social network. It's mainly used by young people for messaging other young people and sometimes following big brands and celebrities they truly 'love'. Your business wouldn't go round sending SMS text messages to teenagers, so why would you use Snapchat? How would they even find you? If you don't have an existing channel or relationship to tell them your user name you'll be fighting a losing battle.

It won't go away. Users who signed up before Instagram expanded its feature set will likely stick with it, but anyone coming AFTER that will probably spend more time on Instagram, or increasingly, TikTok. Social networking platforms are all free, but they do take up our time, and you have to draw the line somewhere. You can't commit to a presence on every platform. For me, Snapchat is where I draw the line.

Gary thinks:

Not a great deal if I'm honest. So let me go ask my teenage son. Ok, he says (and I quote): 'We call it Snap now Dad. It's convenient. It's good for group chats and sharing funny pictures'[33].

I cannot add much to that. I've seen some businesses try and establish a presence on it, either by joining in, and sharing silly pictures and daft selfies with dog ears on (usually ending up looking ridiculous, and being mocked by the users who know it's anything but authentic), or by using the custom geo-filters, targeting a specific area with some funny brand message which the users can choose to embrace (or not).

The latter route is certainly in my opinion a 'safer' option. Let the people be daft and silly while helping spread your fun brand values, rather than you trying to play along, and 'be down with the kids'.

!GeekAlert

Custom GeoFilters is a paid feature on Snapchat which allows anyone (even those not publishing Snaps themselves) to pay a relatively small amount of money to have a 'filter' they have designed (essentially a frame around a 'selfie' with a message or some branding around it) appear to Snapchat users at a particular location at a time of their choosing.

The 'GeoFencing' capability is impressive, meaning you can target a whole city, a football stadium, or just your own office. Anybody in that location (over a dictated period of time) will now see your custom filter, and can apply it to their own pictures before sending to their friends.

If you're going to give this a go, we recommend you go easy on the branding, unless you're a brand they already love. Why would a teenager add your corporate logo to their snap? They might, however, add your filter if it gives them a funny hat, costume, or cool relevant quote to enhance their selfie pout. Think fun and you might succeed.

---

[33] Trust me - that was more than I thought I'd get from him at 10.47 on a Saturday morning.

TikTok

If there's a single social platform that keeps Facebook founder Mark Zuckerberg up at night, we reckon this is the one. From a standing start, TikTok, originally known as Musica.ly and owned by Chinese firm Bytedance, enjoyed huge growth through 2019 and now has well over a billion users.

It's a hybrid bite size video / music discovery platform; a strange mix of Snapchat, Instagram and YouTube. Users of Twitter's short lived 'Vine' video service will feel familiar with elements of it. The user base is typically younger – think teens and early twenty-somethings – but as we saw in the early days of Facebook, this is becoming more general all the time as others discover what they like about it and join themselves.

Dance, pranks, comedy, challenges and memes account for some of the most popular and 'typical' TikTok content, but stick around long enough and you'll discover all sorts. Much of it, in no more than 15 second chunks, although sometimes these can be stitched together to form longer clips of 60 seconds and longer material created elsewhere can be uploaded to your profile.

It's easy to dismiss as a platform where 'kids go to play' but there was a time we might have said that about Facebook and Instagram. Many of the businesses we work with don't use TikTok yet but it's on their radar and they're keeping an eye on it.

We reckon TikTok style videos will go on to influence much of our online communication through the next decade, even if the app itself gets banned in specific countries, taken over by another company or simply copied by Facebook's recently launched Instagram Reels feature.

Top TikTok Tips[34]

1. Download the app.
Download the TikTok app and you can start browsing the content without having to register or create an account. Keep in mind some of it might not be safe for work.

---

[34] Easy for you to say.....

2. Choose the TikTok face of your business carefully.

There's no long form written content on TikTok such as you might find on Twitter and Facebook. It's video or nothing. But there might be someone already working in your team who inherently 'gets it' and understands how to create suitable TikTok style content, that can still deliver a return for your business. This might be an opportunity for someone further down the corporate ladder (a Modern Apprentice or intern for example) to be given some responsibility and allowed to use their creativity to engage a new audience for you on this emerging platform. Don't feel your CEO, MD or even your marketing team has to 'front' every piece of content you put out.

3. Be prepared to play.

Hardly anyone uploads a 'straight' video to TikTok. The overwhelming majority have several fast cuts, different angles, edits, overlays, graphics, and special effects. Look at some and you'll see what we mean. You don't need particularly advanced editing skills to create these either, the majority are built into the TikTok app and are available as templates. Choose whatever you like and be creative. Getting your point across in a fun and creative way within 15 seconds might seem daunting but there are some great tools and techniques which can help you. And don't be too proud to learn from others. Jumping on trends is a huge part of what makes this platform popular. So, if you see someone doing something you like, copy it! But maybe with your own unique spin.

Colin thinks:

God I feel old. Should the over 30s even be on TikTok? Should business be there? Do you want to post videos of you doing the shuffle dance or taking part in a meme about how many sexual partners you've had? I believe young people need, and deserve, a space that is truly their own. There has to be an engine of creativity and self-expression, free from their parents and businesses trying to sell. Can't there be a social network just for 'the younger ones'? Why does it always have to be commercialised? That's part of how I feel about TikTok. The users don't really want me and my business there. That said, anytime I look at TikTok I enjoy it. It seems to be a fun, largely positive space. Spend a few minutes browsing and you'll gain tremendous insight into youth culture. That could be very valuable to your business. The hyper short-form video content forces you to think about how you would explain what you do in an entirely new and visual way. It's a fast moving, exciting place and even if you never post a video yourself under your business name, there are definite benefits to spending time exploring TikTok.

Quick tip: if nothing else, sign up and take your name and your business name as user names. It'll mean if you ever do want to use TikTok it'll be much easier for people to find you.

The numbers alone and the growth it's seeing make it inevitable that TikTok will become, much like Facebook, a place where businesses DO want to be. Look at Dr Julie Smith and Ryerson DMZ – two examples of good business-related TikTok accounts.

Gary thinks:

I cannot NOT be impressed with the numbers behind TikTok. It's been the most downloaded app for months now (especially during the COVID-19 lockdown) and the user growth has been unbelievable. That said, I still have reservations about using this as a business platform.

Firstly, as Colin rightly asks, should this creative, organic, mainly 'young people's platform' be crashed by businesses looking to exploit and sell to them?

Secondly, there are still some 'concerns' about the ties between TikTok and the Chinese government. Authorities from countries such as the USA and India have banned (or are considering banning) people from using it, considering it a national security threat.

Now, I'm not suggesting that you (or your kids) shouldn't use it because Trump doesn't trust it, but it's worth being aware that there are some confirmed reports of data and content passing through (and being stored on?) Chinese servers with likely government access[35].

---

[35] Not that I'd imagine President Xi Jinping really cares much about your fun dance moves while lip synching to Old Town Road.

And lastly, I won't lie, but the few times I've logged into TikTok, I don't just feel old – I feel like an old pervert! It seems to be full of young boys and girls, sometimes scantily dressed, overly sexualised and singing provocative songs. It's not just that of course not, but for me it's certainly not a place a middle-aged man (no matter how cool I still think I am!) wants to consider marketing his business on.

But things change. TikTok will evolve. And it won't be long before (like most of the platforms to date) they're looking to entice businesses in their droves, to exploit their users through advertising, sponsorship, creative partnerships, social influencers, and other ways that commercial organisations can take advantage of, bringing in the marketing money as a result. So while you won't see me busting my moves on TikTok anytime soon, I'll still be keeping a keen eye on where things go in the future.

!GeekAlert

Find a post you've enjoyed on TikTok. Click on the audio icon right at the bottom of the post and you'll be taken to a page featuring every other video using that same audio. You can also use the audio to make your own video.

If the audio you would like to use isn't already on TikTok, play it from another smartphone or sound system while you're recording your video and TikTok will add it to its library.

Another tip: when a user logs into TikTok, they are presented with a 'For You Page' which curates the content TikTok believes they are most likely to enjoy seeing. Having your post appear on someone else's 'For You Page' greatly increases the chances of it being seen and helps you grow a following.

TikTok doesn't comment on how it decides which material ends up on anyone's 'For You Page' but a huge number of users believe using the hashtags #FYP or #ForYouPage increases their chances and so you will see this on a multitude of posts and adding it to your own certainly wouldn't do any harm.

Summing Up

The above is not a definitive list by any measure, with new social platforms (and reincarnations of old ones) appearing all the time. Our workshop discussions usually include some nostalgic throwbacks to Bebo, MySpace and Friends ReUnited, while also debating the 'Is it social?' question in relation to Tinder, Glassdoor and even Amazon[36].

One thing we always like to stress – the platforms are all different.

They attract different audiences, who use them in different ways, with different expectations from them. Some businesses (far too many!) ignore this, and use 'shortcut' tactics to blast the same marketing messages across all of them en masse.

The same message sent to a 19 year old student on Instagram, a 39 year old cafe owner on Facebook, and a 57 year old senior procurement manager on LinkedIn[37]. If that's your approach, don't expect to win any marketing awards any time soon.

Not only are the people (and their behaviours) different across all the platforms, crucially, the technical constraints are different too.

Why limit a LinkedIn post to 280 characters because you've worked out how to auto-post your Tweets to multiple platforms? Do you realise that your #hashtags are fine on Instagram, but when Insta-shared to Pinterest they do nothing (other than annoy Pinterest users who know you're 'cheating' and not really sharing valuable content for them). Possibly the biggest danger is @tagging someone on one platform, automatically cross-posting the message to a different platform, where said person is using a different username! Who have you actually just tagged?

The platforms are different, so don't treat them all the same. Strategic

---

[36] Our view is simple; if it's an online platform where you are influenced by other people, then it's arguably a social network. So even the likes of Amazon – where people are influenced by 'ratings and reviews' written by other consumers – then it too has to be considered social. More on this later!

[37] Other stereotypes are available.

usage of the right platform, helping you achieve your business objectives, by reaching the right audience in the right way, and you might be onto a winner.

Take a 'Say it and Spray it' approach?[38] Good luck.

!GeekAlert

We're not saying don't cut corners, and we fully understand the time pressures faced by most small business owners. But only use automation tactics when it really helps, and consider very carefully how you do it.

One system that Gary especially loves is 'If This Then That' - https://bit.ly/etsbook-ifttt

It's a really clever (and very geeky) site which allows you to connect and join up all your social platforms and various cloud systems.

Some simple things you could do (again, with due consideration) is to have your social media profile pictures all kept in sync, so a change of your Twitter profile, automatically updates your Facebook profile etc. Or you could automatically upload all your Instagram photos into a Facebook album or Pinterest board.

IFTTT can do all this and so much more, and if you start looking at connecting things, such as your Dropbox account, Slack channels, favourite CRM tools, online calendars and more, then you can achieve some pretty cool (and sometimes useful!) data automation and improved efficiency in how you do your marketing.

Or you can do what Gary does, which is connect everything and anything just because he can. When you ring his 'video doorbell', his living room lights flash, and if he doesn't answer you within 15 seconds, your image is Tweeted to a private account, while saved to his cloud drive.

Technically, very impressive. As for Gary's chat at dinner parties?.....Mmmmm.....

---

[38] I don't really know what that means, but I heard Colin say it once and it sounded cool.

What's the next big thing?

A question we're always asked.

Harsh but true – if you're reading this chapter hoping to get a jumpstart on the next cool tool to focus your efforts on, you're likely already too late. If you don't know why a platform is fast becoming the next big thing among your target customers, then you've missed the boat already.

Maybe get yourself a teenager. They can be a bit moody at times but useful for explaining what's cool in the world of social. In fact, no maybes – definitely get yourself a teenager; someone who can challenge your views and look at your business (and how it communicates) from a completely different perspective to your own. Invest in the future and take on a Modern Apprenticeship – provide training and get them formally qualified in all things digital marketing: a career opportunity for them, and a breath of fresh air and creative enthusiasm for you.

Our goal with this book is not to turn anybody into a Facebook or TikTok 'expert'. It's also not to predict the future. Instead our aim is to encourage you to embrace a more social attitude. The tools will come and go. Your customers will decide which ones they like, and which ones they don't. Regardless of your own personal opinions – follow the customers, and be social.

CHAPTER IN A TWEET

There are many different social platforms, attracting different audiences, with different expectations. Respect these differences. Prioritise which platforms will help achieve your objectives, learn how best to use them, and understand what your customers actually want from you on them.

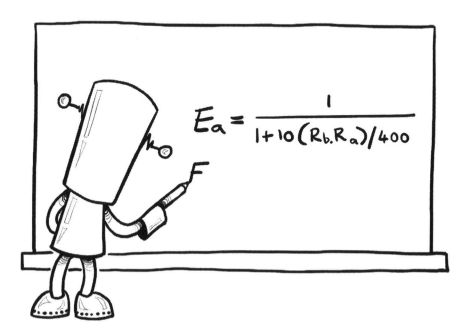

04

$$E_a = \frac{1}{1+10^{(R_b . R_a)/400}}$$

The dreaded social media algorithms

(and why it's no longer just a numbers game)

Colin

In the 'old days' (after Bullseye but before Scot Squad) most social media platforms organised content in reverse chronological order. There was a bit more to it, but in general, the news feed on most major platforms displayed content from the people you followed with the most recent stuff at the top and the most dated material at the bottom.

And even today, if you want your news feed to display content in this order you can still have that, by accessing the settings and selecting your preference.

The vast majority of people stick with the default, and that's where there has been a big change in recent years.

Why we have an algorithm

Facebook decided, and the others followed suit, that their users would be better served (and spend more time using the platforms) if they saw more of the content they liked the most. So, if there's a particular friend I am connected to on Facebook and I always read their content, respond to it and interact with them, I'll see more of it and friends who publish content I regularly ignore and scroll past, I'll see less and less of, until, eventually, they don't appear in my news feed at all. We're still 'Friends', we're still connected, and if these are business pages then I've still 'Liked' the page, it's just that Facebook has decided to stop showing me their posts in my news feed, because it's concluded, based on my actions on Facebook, that I am not interested in this material.

The system Facebook uses to determine what content to show each user in their news feed is an algorithm. It's a series of calculations that give each piece of content a 'score'. In very simplistic terms, the higher the score, the more likely the post will appear in someone's feed.

What this means for you

Back to the 'old days' then and most businesses using Facebook could be pretty confident that if they had, say for example, 500 people who had 'Liked' their business page, then give or take a few, 500 people would see their next post on Facebook.

Now, with the algorithm at work, the audience for that post is often nowhere near 500 or whatever number of likes a business page has. I repeat – just growing the number of likes on your business page is no longer any guarantee of success.

Research suggests the average reach for a post from a business page on Facebook is now 6% of the total number of likes. And of that 6%, what proportion would actually read the post and take action on it, e.g. click the link or call the number? Well, depressingly, the research tells us it's likely to be in the region of 4% of the 6%.

So as you can see, getting any sort of positive result from Facebook has become extremely difficult for many businesses. If you're using Facebook (or any social network) for business, you're publishing content but nothing much is happening, and it's starting to feel as though you're talking to yourself, then I hate to disappoint you but you probably are.

The good news

Don't despair though, we're here to help and in a few moments, Gary is going to share his amazing, ninja level plan to 'Beat The Algorithm'. But first, it's worth taking some time to explore a little more about how it works.

We'll focus on Facebook's algorithm because it is the most powerful of them all and most of the other platforms operate in a similar manner.

The algorithm in practice

We've established that the aim of the news feed algorithm is to give each individual more of the content they want. How does Facebook know what you want? By studying your actions.

For example, let's say you have a friend on Facebook who you regularly private message. You regularly meet face to face. You often talk about that person and anytime you see their content you hit the 'Like' button, often add a comment underneath and regularly 'share' the post with your other friends. Facebook takes all this as a pretty clear sign that you appreciate the content this particular friend shares and want more of it. And so, it gives you more and if you react in the same way to that content, you'll see even more, and so on and so on.

At the other extreme, there's a friend you are connected to who you don't appreciate so much. They share posts that you don't even stop scrolling for in your news feed. As I'm sure you've concluded, quickly, Facebook will stop showing you their content in your news feed. If you go looking for it, on their page, for example, you'll still find it, and if you start liking, or reacting to it in any way, commenting and sharing it, then very quickly, their subsequent posts will start to appear throughout your news feed.

It's exactly the same for any posts your business page shares and the people who have LIKED you. The fact they 'liked' the page some time ago, counts for very little. It's the engagement Facebook is looking at. If content doesn't get any reaction – likes, comments, shares, link clicks, video views, etc. – then pretty quickly Facebook will assume that the content is boring, unwanted and will stop showing it to your followers in their news feeds.

There are well over 200 criteria Facebook's algorithm takes into account. Likes, comments and shares (engagement) are perhaps the most powerful, but others include 'time decay' (how long it's been since this post was published), and 'post type', that is, basically, how much effort you've gone to when publishing this post and does Facebook appreciate what you're trying to do.

For example, Gary told me some time ago that I should write a blog. So I did. I published a blog post on my website then came to my Facebook page and shared the link. It looked something like this:

JUST BLOGGED: Why customer service
is your new best friend:
www.embracethespacebook.com

8	0
People Reached	Engagements

As you can see, that post was seen by eight people.

Eight people??! That's awful!

There are more than eight people in this coffee shop where I'm writing this right now. I don't need Facebook at all if it's only going to get this blog in front of eight people! What a waste of time. In fact, hang on, I'm going to shout my blog to everyone that's in this branch of Caffè Nero. I'll show Facebook......

I'm now writing the rest of this section from a bench in George Square after being asked to leave Caffè Nero for shouting.

Anyway, in that post above I'd committed a cardinal sin in Facebook's eyes. I was using Facebook to try to take people away from Facebook and onto my website. Facebook doesn't like that. Its entire business model aims to keep people on Facebook all day long if it can. And so when I come along, and share a quick link to my blog, Facebook responds by showing that post to as small a number of people who have liked my page as it can. My biggest fans will see it, the people who have liked my page and gone on to interact with my content the most. If they find it engaging – if they click the link, like, comment, and best of all, share the post – then even though Facebook doesn't like what I'm trying to do, it will heed the signals from the audience, assume this content is valuable and something people want, and show it to more people. As they react and engage with it, the process continues and if it was an exceptionally exciting blog that stimulated a great reaction, then the total reach could end up even exceeding the total number of 'Likes' my page has achieved.

In reality, what happened in the example above, was Facebook showed the post to some of my biggest fans, the people most likely to engage with the things I say, and none of them did.

Facebook interprets that lack of engagement as confirmation that this was indeed a boring post that nobody wants to read. And so I am punished for that. It shows the post about my blog to as small a number of people as possible and if it doesn't get a positive response, it will go no further. It still exists on my page, it just doesn't show up in anyone else's news feed.

Let's look at another post.

Here's John, one of the best bosses I ever worked with. What qualities make a great leader? And who is the most inspirational leader you've ever worked for? Let me know in the comments.

349
People Reached

14
Engagements

First, I get a reward from Facebook for including a picture. It knows audiences like posts with pictures so straight away, this is going to be seen by a few more people than it would have been if it was plain text. Next, Facebook knows I'm asking a question. Questions need answers, answers equal engagement and what Facebook is hoping for here is that a comment thread develops with a range of opinions that people will take time to read and interact with. All that adds up to more time spent on Facebook, which, as we've explained, is Facebook's (or any social network's) primary goal. So the reward I get for that, is the post being pushed out to more and more people. And every comment received counts as further engagement and the audience will increase even further.

Finally, here's a post where I shared some video.

In this post, I'm giving Facebook its favourite form of content. Video. Notice this is not a link to a YouTube video or video on my website. This is a video uploaded directly to Facebook. Facebook wants to become the home of video on the internet. It knows audiences love watching video content on their smartphone, so if you give Facebook video content, you get suitably rewarded. And the reward is, more people see your stuff.

We've spoken about Facebook here but I can't stress enough that Instagram, Twitter, LinkedIn, Pinterest and all the rest operate in a similar way. Just as Google determines what the first page of search results looks like, (and it'll be different for everyone) these social networks have built their businesses by controlling how each of our news feeds are organised.

A few key points to remember:

> Effort is rewarded. Plain text is out. Everything should have pictures and/ or video.

> How long has it been since you posted? If I log in at 9pm and your most recent post was earlier that day at 10am, there's a high chance it's going to be regarded as 'old news' and unless it's achieved some serious engagement, I'm unlikely to see it.

> External links are penalised. Unless it's essential content everyone wants to click and read, Facebook isn't in the business of sending traffic to your website. So instead of sharing a link to your blog, could you re-write the blog as a Facebook post? Or upload a short video of you discussing key points from your blog? The more you can do on Facebook (or whatever platform you're using) and the more you can make use of its full feature set, the easier it's going to be for you to reach an audience.

There. I hope that wasn't too painful. Now you understand the basics of what the algorithm is and why it matters, here comes Gary to share with you his ninja tips on how to beat the algorithm.

CHAPTER IN A TWEET

Thanks to the social media algorithms, organic reach is getting less and less. The average for Facebook business pages is now just 6%. Posting more engaging content (like video), starting discussions, and minimising external links, will all help to turn things around.

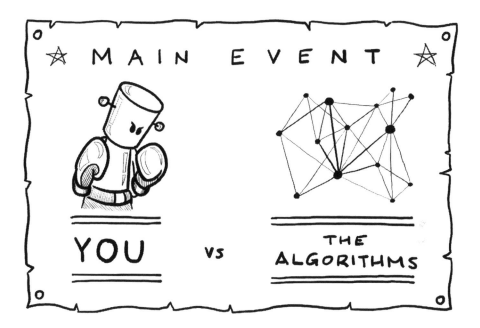

05

How to beat the algorithms

(with some knock-out engagement tactics)

Gary

Now that Colin has explained a little more about how these social media algorithms work, let's take a look at some practical measures to help fight back against them.

Actually, before we do that, let's remind ourselves why they exist: to provide a better user experience for the billions of people actually using these platforms.

Despite the fact that we, as business owners and marketeers, might lament the algorithms (trust me, I've attended enough social media conferences, and there's usually a talk entitled 'The Damned Algorithms') what we cannot forget is the fact they are there for the good of the people.

While we all might like to believe that Mr Zuckerberg is limiting our 'free' reach on Facebook in order to make more billions (which is of course partly true), the reason why Facebook is hiding content left right and centre is because it has to! There's too much content.

As a user of Facebook you (and everyone else too) cannot see everything; you've got too many friends, like too many businesses, follow too many celebrities and politicians (maybe start your cull there?), and when they all post updates, the algorithm has to decide what to show you. And it's making decisions based on what it genuinely thinks you want (or don't want) to see. So before you go about trying to 'game' the systems, don't forget the basics – provide content that people truly want to see, and you'll do just fine (follow the Golden Rules from earlier).

But as a business, even with the best ideas, sharing content that you're certain your customers will love, those pesky algorithms just keep getting in the way. At this point I should probably highlight my love for spell-checkers. My spelling of the word algorithm would differ wildly across this whole chapter if it wasn't auto-corrected.

While you'll never fully beat them, here are five strategies that we know help businesses achieve more reach, and improve your chances of making the cut.

Engagement

We've mentioned this word already in the book (many times!) and the truth is, if you were only going to take away just one thing having read it cover to cover (and we hope you'll get more than one nugget!) then it should be this. Engagement is arguably the measure that matters most across all your social channels, as it's one of the biggest signals to the platforms that people actually care about your content.

So what that you've got 10,000 likes says Facebook, nobody actually engages with you. They liked your business page, but clearly they don't really like you or your content. If that's the scenario, watch your 'Reach' plummet.

A like on your status update proves that somebody actually took the time to read it, and deem it worthy of a response. Granted there's not much effort in clicking the 'thumbs up' icon (or any of the other icons that makeup the 'reactions') but it's something, and something is better than nothing.

A comment takes even more effort from your reader, and again this is recognised as a sign of value; they've bothered to reply to you, add in their tuppence, continue the discussion thread from which more might follow.

And if they share your post – watch those numbers rise! Your content is so good, so valuable, so funny, so 'engaging'......that I'll share it with my friends. Not only do you get to reach their wider circles, but the algorithm gives you a boost across the board.

Remember that engagement essentially means anything other than scrolling on by. Most content (assuming it actually appears in my news feed) gets scrolled on by. I don't even see it (more on how to improve that later), and it makes no lasting impact whatsoever. The social platforms recognise that you've scrolled on, and make a note to not bother you with that type of content (or worse, content from that business) in the future.

Even someone pausing for a few extra milliseconds (compared to everything else they've scrolled past) is a signal of engagement. Likes, comments and shares might be the most obvious (and easily counted) engagement measures, but equally important are 'eyeball time', image enlargements, videos watched, links clicked and anything else that involves them 'doing something' with your content.

So a big part of your social media strategy is asking yourself the question: 'How can I get more engagement?'. Because if you're not getting any, there's arguably no point in posting.

Typically, the question results in two streams of thought. Achieving higher levels of engagement through better content. And achieving more engagement through clever 'technical' tips and tricks.

When it comes to content, we'll look at this in much more detail in the next chapter, but here's an interesting statistic from research carried out from the New York Times a few years ago:

> **❝** 84% of people share social media content because it's a way to support causes or issues they care about.[39] **❞**

Based on this, you'll get extra engagement (and therefore reach) because you're posting up things you genuinely believe your audience will care about. Content which resonates with them, means something, and shows some shared values between you and them.

As for technical tips and tricks, here's a few to get you started:

❯ Do you even try to get the audience to engage with you? A simple example of this is the typical 'Happy Friday' post. At the very least make it slightly better by giving yourself a chance of user engagement: 'Happy Friday – what are your plans for the weekend?'. Ask, don't tell, is a good strategy, and often elicits a response (simply because you asked for one).

❯ Images and video generally provide a more engaging post. The brain reacts differently to images (than to words), and often the visual nature of your content is what stops someone to glance further at it. In years gone

---

[39] https://bit.ly/etsbook-nytimes

by, Colin and I used to advise businesses to 'Try and include an image'......
now we hint that there's no choice but to. Not if you want a result from
it. That said, be careful about your choice of image, especially if just
picking from a list of GIFs or stock photos. An image is worth a thousand
words (or so the adage goes), and sometimes people interpret them with
different words to those you intended.

> Are you talking about someone (or some business) in particular? Could you
@tag them in your post? If you do, they'll almost certainly be notified about
it, and that might bring an easy first like or share. Tag another account only
when it's relevant, don't just 'spam tag' anyone and everyone!

> Are you posting at the right time of day? Depending on your audience,
engagement rates will differ based on posting the content at a suitable
time of the day (or night) that best suits. That is, the time they are most
likely to be online (using that platform) with the ability to engage back
with you. Check your analytics and insights and you might just spot a
missed opportunity to reach them at the perfect time.

> Mix it up. Have you fallen into the habit of posting typical 'text and an
image' content? If yes, take some time to explore the many options that
Facebook (and others) give you. Consider polls, events (be creative – a
'50% off sale' can easily be promoted as an event), offers and specific
calls to action to drive more engagement, but don't forget Colin's advice
from earlier: be careful about trying to always take people off the social
network onto your own website. Could you instead try and keep them
on? Start a Q&A, highlight an opinion, or broadcast live video. Which
leads me to our second strategy to beat the algorithms......

Do more videos!

Videos are HOT right now, with more people than ever before consuming
video content across all the popular social channels.

According to HubSpot, social media posts with video have 48% more views.
It's not just the users of the platforms that want your videos, it's the platforms

themselves. A good rule of thumb to remember is this: if content is good for the platform, it's good for you. Facebook (and others) want more videos because it knows (from the big data it has available to it) that people like it. If they like it, they watch more of it, and if they watch more of it (and that's what the data tells us!) then they stay longer on Facebook doing so. How does Facebook make its money? By having as many people as possible stay as long as possible. Give Facebook your videos, and they reward you by increasing your reach so that everyone benefits!

At the time of writing this, Facebook content containing a video (and I stress, by video, we mean an actual video file, uploaded direct to Facebook, not just a link to a YouTube video) receives on average twice the audience engagement (when compared to other posts). Live Video even more!

It's a no brainer – video content works, and helps battle back against the algorithm. It's by no means just Facebook. LinkedIn introduced its own video platform in 2017 (before which you could only link to video on YouTube etc.), and more recently began rolling out Live Video, all for the same reasons as Facebook and others – because users want to watch it. Again, we'll leave it to you to consider what videos you start making, but to try and convince you that there's more than just 'about us' promotional videos (often your least engaged with videos on social platforms), here's a few ideas to consider.

Authoritative videos

A phrase that's been used a fair amount lately, and often part of the many 'digital marketing' workshops on the market. All this really means is content that helps establish you as an 'authority' on a particular subject. Increasingly popular on the likes of LinkedIn, these (often 'head and shoulders') videos help position you as an expert by discussing something relevant to your industry. The principle here is that most others are trying to 'sell stuff', but you're willing to go on camera and 'talk about stuff'. They can be especially powerful if you have an opinion on an industry topic, or share some insight or knowledge (often called 'thought leadership') that others typically keep to themselves, or are even too scared to broach. Share yourself speaking with passion and belief about a particular topic, and the world starts to see you as an expert with real authority.

Behind-the-scenes videos

People like to 'see what they normally don't' – so what's commonplace and run of the mill to you, might be a valuable insight into your business to someone else. An easy example: we're all used to seeing the beautiful finished shiny jewellery from the many small business silversmiths out there, but if they showed me more videos of what goes into making it – the hard graft, the dirty hands, the smolten metal[40] and many hours of blood, sweat and tears – this behind-the-scenes content would have me appreciating the finished piece a whole lot more, and appreciating the business a whole lot more too. Customer 'trust levels' go up the more you bring down walls and let them see inside. What could you showcase that your customers don't normally get to see?

Customer testimonial videos

I'm a huge fan of customer testimonial content full stop (lots more on this in Chapter 10). Most businesses don't do enough to get it, let alone make the most of it. Anything from a happy customer that highlights the value you gave them is powerful marketing. Now more than ever, people are sceptical: 'Why should I believe anything you say? You're a business trying to sell me stuff'. Your customers, however, I trust them a little more. The reviews on your Amazon products, the recommendations on your LinkedIn profile, the rating on your Trust Pilot page. Customer videos are (in my opinion) even more powerful than everything else. Why? Because done right, they are authentic. Anyone could have written those lovely words you feature on your webpage, but not the customer video. As long as you ensure you're getting the right people to record them (not too polished, never scripted, real people), then they could become your best and most impactful marketing content which ironically, isn't YOU doing the marketing. Let someone else tell the world how good you are – the world doesn't believe you anyway.

---

[40] I have no idea if 'smolten metal' is even a thing. My spell-checkers suggests it's not, but hopefully you get my point.

Live videos

I've already hinted at the additional engagement you might get with creating Live videos, so what could you find in your business that's worthy of a live-stream? We return to ideas for live video streaming later in Chapter 7, but the trick is to offer something that's valuable now, not tomorrow or next week; what would the customer want to watch right now? It could be a live event, or Q&A session with a high profile member of staff. Perhaps you're launching a new product, or giving a tour of your facilities. Hosted live, the audience know they can interact, engage, ask questions, and actually steer the video production. With a pre-recorded video, I get to watch, nothing else.

Top Tip: be aware that live videos become 'normal' videos on your social feeds after you're done, so remember that you need to start talking, and welcoming people immediately (even if there's no one watching live at that point). Otherwise, everyone watching tomorrow sees you clearing your throat, checking your hair, and fiddling with the camera settings. People will give up watching it before you actually 'start' on your content, thinking you've accidentally hit record!

!GeekAlert

OBS Studio (free software) allows multi-camera live video streaming from your desktop computer to Facebook or YouTube, with graphic overlays and green screen backgrounds etc. It's a very popular choice for professional live streamers.

ReStream.IO is also worth a look, as it allows you to stream live to multiple channels at the same time, such as Facebook, YouTube, LinkedIn and Twitter.

Use groups

You've probably joined a Facebook (or LinkedIn) group or two over the years, but have you considered actually creating one? I'll simplify the main benefit as follows: post content to your Facebook Business Page (which I've 'liked') and the chances are (due to the algorithm) I won't see it; post content into a Facebook group that I've joined, and the chances are I will see it.

Groups aren't a silver bullet – they are impacted by the algorithm too. But Facebook and LinkedIn essentially take the view that you joined a group for a reason, that is, because you're interested in the group's content and discussions. So suffice to say they are 'favoured' by the algorithms, increasing your chances of your content being seen by those who most want it.

Could you create a group and provide valuable content which encourages people[41] to join it? That's often the biggest challenge – others questioning the value of 'why join this?'. You need to give them a reason, one which benefits THEM, not just you! Just because you get to reach them more easily via the group, you need to consider things from their perspective, turn it on its head, and work out what groups they might WANT to join. I don't want your marketing (we've covered this already!) so what do I want?

Groups that we've seen succeed have included customer support groups (giving users direct access to people that can help)[42], customer VIP groups (treat me like a superstar and give me 'stuff' you don't just give to anyone)[43], niche topic groups (if your organisation has many products/services, then segment customers into groups to super-serve them with relevant content) and digital versions of physical groups (we use them for every cohort of students on our Digital Diploma qualification).

---

[41] Worth mentioning that on Facebook, businesses can join groups too, they're not just for individuals. Perhaps your business could join a few existing groups too if creating one isn't for you yet?

[42] If your customers start using your 'support' groups (because they do actually get better support) then you'll also benefit from the added bonus of taking customer complaints out of the public eye.

[43] One of my favourite examples of this is the VIP 'WhatsApp Group' run by Greggs the Bakers – limited to 250 UK superfans of vegan steakbakes and pastries! I'm not kidding! Google it.

Use stories

For as long as human beings have existed, we've used storytelling to build and strengthen relationships. From ancient clan gatherings round the campfire, to bedtime storybook reading to the kids. Telling stories brings things to life, it humanises otherwise factual information, and presents content in an easy to understand 'relatable' format.

The concept of stories in a social media context has grown hugely over the last few years. Starting with Snapchat (or 'Snap' as the kids call it), the idea was quickly 'borrowed' by Instagram, and then rolled out within Facebook. LinkedIn has also recently launched something very similar (currently being tested in different countries) and at the time of writing, Twitter is trialling its own story-esque content which its calling 'Fleets', as they jump on the story telling bandwagon too!

So what are stories? They are 'secondary content', appearing outwith the main newsfeeds, usually created as short five to 15 second videos, annotated with labels, emojis, hashtags, locations and more. They are transient (or throw-away) pieces of content, typically set to disappear after 24 hours, and they are best for......well......telling stories (the clues in the name!).

Instagram recently confirmed that stories have now overtaken the news feed in terms of reach (based on the volume of people consuming them), yet despite this (and all the trends pointing in one direction), many businesses are still not taking advantage.

Posting a business story allows you to bypass the constraining algorithms of the news feed and have your brand appear 'above it'. With one click I'm viewing your story, and seeing one or more short clips which provide an insight into your day, the event you're currently running, the behind-the-scenes stuff, the flash sale and so on. There are no rules to what you should post, and a good starting point is asking yourself: 'What story do you want to tell?'.

My own story telling usually involves 'a day in the life of' type content, with me posting up daft clips showing the train journey I'm on, or the conference room I'm setting up in. With permission I'll then add a few clips giving a flavour of the workshop, and sometimes make a feature of the smiling (always smiling!) attendees, occasionally giving a quick testimonial or a visual thumbs-up! I'm simply sharing the story of my day, visible for just 24 hours, and then tomorrow it's gone. Fun throw-away, authentic content which hopefully puts a smile on people's faces, and subtly reminds them of what I do! It's Marketing Jim but not as we know it[44].

Paid promotions

If all else fails, and you're still struggling to battle back against the algorithms, there's still one final (failsafe) way to ensure a bigger reach. Pay them!

This strategy deserves a whole chapter to itself, so feel free to jump to Chapter 8 right now if you simply cannot wait.

While the other four strategies above will certainly help you fight back against the social media algorithms, they are still by no means a guaranteed route to success. The social platforms play by their own rules, and while it frustrates business owners that organic reach is getting less and less, they are entitled to make decisions for either the benefit of their users, or (more likely) their stakeholders.

If you want to ensure a guaranteed increase in reach (which remember, is no guarantee of actual engagement, or indeed business success) then understand that the ONLY way to do this is by considering some paid promotions.

The need to 'Pay to Play' should be part of your business thinking. Especially if you're spending marketing money elsewhere and not seeing much of a return. I'm biased of course, but nothing frustrates me more than when I see a business spending money on 'traditional' marketing, such as newspaper or magazine adverts, printed flyers, mainstream media promotions and more, but which still 'rules out' paying for impact on Facebook or Twitter.

---

[44] If your name's not Jim and you're wondering why I called you that, then you need more sci-fi in your life. If your name IS Jim then I hope my clairvoyant capabilities have amazed you.

I'm not saying don't invest in traditional marketing (far from it), but to dismiss the power of paid social media because you begrudge giving Facebook money for what you used to get for free is a short sighted approach.

Paid activity on any social platform, when done correctly, can achieve impressive results. From boosted posts on Facebook to Promoted Pins on Pinterest, targeted advertising (and that's the key – you need to target it) offers a direct and guaranteed route to your chosen market. Even if you've already got these people on your platforms, sometimes the only way we can actually reach them is to get out the company credit card.

Don't begrudge it. Give it a try and you might be pleasantly surprised!

CHAPTER IN A TWEET

Engagement – the most important consideration when it comes to achieving impact on social media and fighting back against the algorithms. More engagement = more reach. Other strategies include more video content, using groups, posting stories and of course, paying them!

#TrainerLife

Go F*!k yourself!

· ·

It's fair to say that on the whole, most of the people we get in front of at workshops, events and conferences etc. are lovely. Most of them are there because they want to be. They want to learn, to be inspired, to grow their businesses or to get better at particular social platforms.

At the risk of trumpet blowing, I'd go so far to say that 99.9% of the many thousands of people we encounter, leave having had an amazing day, with stacks of ideas and inspiration. We see confirmation of this regularly via the feedback sheets and face to face chats with everyone at the end of any session.

But there have been a few interesting attendees who weren't quite so warm and fuzzy.

Like the teenage boy at the School Cyber Conference, who (unknowingly to me) spoiled my otherwise flawless group selfie photo with a perfectly placed middle finger, telling me exactly what he thought of my presentation. This photo[45] ended up being my 'most viral' post of the year, with over 150,000 views in just 48 hours! Some people thought I'd faked the whole thing for effect, but I'm afraid it was real; the lad simply didn't like me, and wanted the world to know it!

Then there was the business owner who attended a practical 'hands on' session, taking it literally and slapping the computer monitor in frustration every time Facebook confused him (which was every few minutes it seemed). This was many years ago, long before COVID-19 concerns, but suffice to say that Colin and I social-distanced ourselves more than two metres that day!

But even more memorable was the girl who shouted out during a small business (public sector funded) training workshop telling me to: "Go F!k Yourself".*

---

[45] Here's what I think of your workshop mister... https://bit.ly/etsbook-finger

Taken aback at this, and certain that I'd misheard her, I simply replied with: "Excuse me?"......to which again, she repeated nice and clearly, telling everyone in the room: "I said.....GO F*!K YOURSELF".

Reflecting on this situation later, I realised that the same girl had earlier asked if there were any 'hand-outs' for the workshops, to which I replied: "No – we supply you with a digital link to the slides later, we're trying to save the trees, feel free to take notes etc. etc."

Was the reason for this later outburst simply based on the fact that I wasn't giving the attendees handouts that day!!? I suspect partly this, and (as it became clear to everyone) partly because of the volume of alcohol she had consumed on the boat while travelling to the venue! You never quite know what's going on in other people's lives, so I certainly won't judge her for it, but thankfully not many people turn up steaming drunk at business events (what they drink during some of the events is another matter!).....

Long story short, the girl was politely and sensitively escorted from the building, and put safely back in a taxi destined for the ferry, and the event continued without further incident. If nothing else it gave everyone some good chat over the coffee break.

Thankfully we DID have coffee for them – if there were no handouts AND no coffee, we'd have had a riot on our hands!

Gary

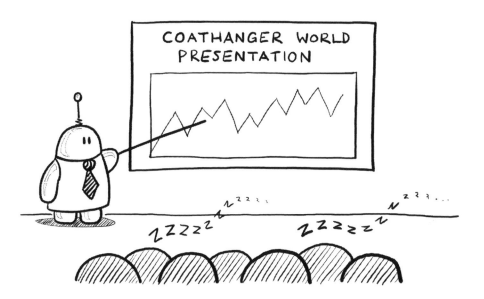

06

Creating
great content
(which stands out from the crowd)

Gary

Content is the lifeblood of a social media strategy. You simply cannot 'do social' without saying something, sharing something, or posting some kind of content with the intention of people seeing it and being influenced by it[46].

Despite what some experts will claim, there's no 'right or wrong' content when it comes to social media. What works for the audience of one business or brand might be considered 'pointless noise' from others. What's important is knowing what works for you. Or more accurately, what works for your audience.

How you measure impact is your choice, but I'd suggest a simple starting point is 'reach': how many people saw the post? In the past we've suggested not using this – just because they saw it, doesn't mean it had any impact.

Nowadays, however, (as we covered earlier when discussing social media algorithms) obtaining organic reach is one of the hardest things to achieve, and often your farthest reaching content, is not surprisingly, your most engaging content. I'd argue that now more than ever, 'reach' could be considered a stamp of approval for quality, or at least an indication that it 'worked' for your audience. Dull, pointless, irrelevant content that doesn't connect with them doesn't tend to achieve much reach. The algorithms make sure of that. Sure, I'd still hope that you have other measures and analytics in place to ensure reach = actual business impact (visit Chapter 15 some ideas), but for now we'll keep it simple.

A nice rule of thumb[47] we've developed over the years is: create content that people see. With social media feeds bursting at the seams with an overload of information, we literally mean that they need to see it. Your content needs to stand out and be seen.

How do you create content people see? You follow our simple 'SEE' acronym[48].

---

[46] That of course is a lie, and you can 'do social' from purely a voyeuristic stance, learning from what you see, while posting nothing yourself.

[47] The origin of that phrase is both fascinating and terrifying in equal measure.

[48] Over the years I've been hugely tempted to further develop this into a 'SEE-SAW' acronym.

S urprise
E ducate
E ntertain

If you're able to post content which achieves just one of these things for your audience, then there's a good chance they'll stop scrolling that busy social feed and pause to take a look. If your content does all three – it's a guaranteed winner!

S - Surprise

People like surprises. Ok, that's not always true – I once received a surprise visit from the VAT man which hardly had me jumping for joy[49]. Like them or not, they are memorable, and they stand out. A surprising bit of content is simply something the viewer was not expecting to see in their feed that day. Something, which by its nature, stands out and evokes a human reaction.

An extreme form of surprise is shock[50] and this is often used to get attention in today's world of marketing when cutting through is increasingly challenging. Think about how the Government convinces you to stick to the speed limit – by showing you TV adverts which hold no punches with regard to the horrific impact of what happens when you speed. Or the animal welfare charities, which ask you for money, while at the same time showing you some horrendous imagery of mistreated pets.

The opposite of surprise is expectation. Content which I expect (usually not in a good way) your type of business to post. Content which I expect to bore me, to advertise to me, to repeat the same marketing message to me, to fade into the background noise and eventually become invisible to me (either by the clever filters in my brain, or because the algorithm knows I don't want it).

E - Educate

If you sell laser pointers (those things you use in training rooms, or for winding up your neighbour's cat), people know when they need them, they understand what they do, and they probably don't care which company they

---

[49] I should state that the random investigation was in fact that, and it resulted in nothing but praise for my financial record keeping and VAT procedures.
[50] Thankfully, another 'S', so my aide memoir still holds true.

buy them from (most likely heading straight to Amazon, and re-ordering a laser pointer device by either price or ratings).

But many other products and services require an explanation. You have to spend time getting the customer to the point where they understand what it could actually do for them, helping them decide they want it, want it from you, and want it now. An accountant might be an example. Or ditching your laptop and using a Chromebook. Or why should someone come to a particular training session?

This is where you have to educate your customers, and one of the ways to do this is to give away some of your 'best stuff' for free. Tell them a bit about saving money on their tax return. Show them the sorts of things a good accountant does. Explain why a Chromebook actually is capable of working without a wifi internet connection. Take them inside the training session and highlight some of the things they're going to learn. The trick is to establish trust with the potential customer. To change their mindset so they understand the benefits they're going to get if they go ahead and make a purchase. It's also about establishing yourself as the expert. In the minds of your audience, they should be so impressed with what they are learning from the free material on your social media channels, that they are more than happy to pay in order to get the full 'premium' experience.

Never give away 'free stuff' with little or no value. Otherwise you've just associated yourself with over-promising, under-delivering, and wasting my time. But if you truly understand me, (remember Point 2 from our Golden Rules earlier?), understand my life, my values, my problems, and my 'objections to the sale'[51], then you'll stop trying to sell to me. Instead you'll educate me. You'll have me wanting to learn more. And you'll have cleverly positioned yourself as a business who cares and tries to help, rather than as a business who just sells.

A final example might be a business that sells sheds. If I am looking for more space to work from home, I might consider moving to a bigger house, or

---

[51] If you've even been on a sales training course you'll have heard that phrase. It essentially just means the reasons people use to justify not buying your product or services. Too expensive being the most common response, but often there's so many other reasons that business owners fail to understand.

converting my attic. Buying a shed might be the furthest thing from my mind because I know nothing about sheds and I've never considered it. Maybe when I think of sheds I think of the kind my Dad had in the early 80s. They've changed a lot since then. So the shed company educates me about how to work effectively from home, and in doing so, is careful to mention how a shed can be part of that solution. The key with this approach is to focus on helping me – giving me advice and information, supporting me as I look to work from home, rather than only being concerned with selling me a shed.

I don't want a shed. So pricing, or a discount isn't going to help. But as you educate me more about working from home, and how a shed is an affordable, cost effective, free from planning permission alternative to a home extension[52] (and that they look awesome), then I start to see the shed as a possible solution and I'm already in the right place to consider buying one.

This approach goes right back to our Golden Rules. If we know our audience, then we should know what they care about, which leads to a better understanding of how we can help them. You're also playing a numbers game, where the odds are usually in your favour. According to Google Trends, prior to the COVID-19 outbreak, UK Google searches for the phrase 'How to work from home?' out-numbered searches for 'buy a shed' roughly four to one. Just after the start of lockdown, it was 20 to one. Simply put, way more people want to know more about working from home than are looking to buy sheds today[53]. So if you're trying to sell sheds, start getting smarter.

Jay Baer (author and online customer service expert) says it best in one of his videos:

> **66** The difference between helping and selling is only two letters. But those letters make all the difference in modern business. Because if you *sell* to someone, you create a customer today. If you *help* someone, you create a customer for life.[54] **99**

---

[52] Please seek professional advice to check that your future shed doesn't need planning permission.
[53] Good luck trying to sell sheds in Northern Ireland. Zero searches on Google apparently!
[54] Watch the full Jay Baer video here: https://bit.ly/etsbook-jaybaer

Create educational content you know will help your audience, and they'll see it, value it, and remember that it was you who provided it. It might not lead to immediate sales, but it helps build trust, which builds relationships, which hugely increases the chances of business further down the line.

E - Entertain

People don't use social media with the express intention of hanging on every word of your business. What got them on the platform in the first place was interacting with the people they care about, getting information they need, and having fun. Consider your own use of social media – the things you like, comment on and share. I'm going to guess it's generally not the annual report from your favourite local authority. It's probably something lighter, something a bit fun. Maybe even a cat video (the one where it chases the laser pointer).

We aren't all natural born entertainers (well, maybe Kevin Bridges is), but there are things that happen every day, inside your business, that when shared properly, can be entertaining enough to achieve engagement. We don't need edge-of-your-seat drama or side-splitting comedy, just something that might brighten our day and lead us to make a connection. Just making your business more human, naturally makes it more entertaining. And you should look for opportunities to achieve this. People are a great place to start.

If you have staff, who are the characters in your business? What are their hobbies, interests and hidden talents? What behind-the-scenes discussions go on in your workplace? Could you share some of that with the outside world?

One fashion retailer we worked with made a star out of the delivery guy that brought the new clothes in each week. He began appearing in their videos, singing, dancing, sharing 'thoughts for the day' – the audience loved him!

There's a temptation sometimes to make you (the business owner) the focus of everything. You don't need to be. Look at who is on reception, the modern apprentice, the window cleaner.....the office dog. There is entertainment and fun all around, you just have to identify it and then share it on your social channels in a way that entertains the audience AND somehow helps the business at the same time.

The need for visuals

Here's a quote I never imagined including in this book:

> 66 The soul never thinks without an image 99
> **Aristotle**

Learning the art of making your content visual is one of the most important skills you can develop. Images and videos elicit emotional responses in people – and a wee reminder, it's people who you're trying to have look at (and respond to) your content.

I'm not saying you shouldn't use text, but be careful about using too much of it and always try and bring it to life with visuals. Lots of geeky research finds that people's attention spans are getting increasingly shorter (you'll likely have seen the facts about fish having longer attention spans than we do), and this is backed up with data from the platforms themselves which prove that shorter, more concise posts tend to get more engagement than longer alternatives. Instead of going with your '10 ideas to increase productivity' post on LinkedIn, why not try breaking it down into ten smaller posts, each with just one idea, and each illustrated with an image. Or perhaps turn it into a digestible listicle (yes, that is a word) accompanied by a short video reinforcing your key points.

Some businesses are fortunate, they are already visual. If you produce physical products, or go to interesting places, the good quality images and video clips will take care of themselves. But if you provide a service, such as financial consulting or mental health counselling, where clients would like a degree of privacy, or where your business 'looks' quite boring or corporate, then creating engaging visuals is going to be much harder.

Remember though that the images don't have to be photographs of real, live human beings. They could be graphics or illustrations. You could use a tool such as Canva (photo editing software with a very good free version) to manipulate an image, include calls to action, size it correctly through the various digital channels and tell a complete story through images rather than text. This would immediately make your social media much more interesting and engaging.

Research shows that audiences much prefer pictures and video on social media compared to plain text. There's concrete proof that visual posts achieve greater results in platform algorithms, so it's well worth taking some time to develop your image creation skills, and consider how you can achieve good quality images that tell the story of your business in a way that people actually see and care about.

Remember also that most people consume your content on their mobile phone. What works really well as an A4 poster on your shop window won't work as a digital image on your customers' Facebook feeds. Ensure that what you create is suitable for mobile devices, and if you're using text overlays, check that people can actually read it (on their 2.5 inch wide screen).

!GeekAlert

One of the most popular tools for creating social media graphics right now is Canva.com. This is a 'freemium' product which many people never pay a penny for (since the capability of the free version is pretty amazing). Canva turns everyone into a designer[55], with customisable templates, drag and drop features, and a tonne of inspiration. If you've not created an account already, get it done!

Other cool tools for graphics include Layout and Boomerang (two mobile apps from Instagram), Quik for creating simple high energy videos, and Adobe Spark Post or Ripl for animated graphics and adverts.

Whatever tools you choose, just get on with taking (or making) more photos and short videos. Don't find yourself in the situation today where you wish you'd taken photos of that event yesterday. Your mobile phone in your pocket is capable of some amazing photos and videos, so long as you remember to get it out of your pocket and actually take them. Get into that habit, and start capturing footage, ensuring you're never short of a visual when you need one.

---

[55] Designers will of course have a different view.

Let me finish this chapter by sharing a conversation I had over breakfast with my son a few years ago. He was six years old at the time.

Jamie: What's Facebook Dad?

Dad: What do you think it is?

Jamie: A place where people can put stuff up for other people to see.

Dad: What kind of stuff?

Jamie: Special stuff.

Dad: Why?

Jamie: So others can give it a 'tick'.

Dad: Why do they do that?

Jamie: Because they've nothing else to do?

Dad: Exactly!

As a business looking for impact, always try and post 'special stuff'. Stuff that people actually give a damn about. But don't just post it because you've got nothing better to do. Posting just for the sake of it only adds to all the digital noise, usually resulting in content that nobody cares about. Meaning nobody sees it. Good content takes time, consideration, planning, creativity and a real understanding of your intended audience. Back to golden rule number three: 'Give them something they want to share'. Stick to that, and you'll definitely get more ticks!

CHAPTER IN A TWEET

Creating engaging content which people 'SEE' will help you stand out in crowded news feeds. Content which Surprises, Educates or Entertains your audience, brought to life with strong images or videos, will help your business achieve more.

07

Live streaming, webinars and video conferencing

(and why digital 'face to face' still matters)

Colin

For reasons I've never quite understood, many businesses in the UK have always seemed a bit reluctant to fully embrace remote working, which is strange given our position floating around on an island. My Dad worked from home in his HR job back in the mid-90s, with an ISDN line but still made regular trips to Staines for meetings with colleagues! Some of us haven't really moved on much since then. A couple of years ago, a client of mine in London called me up and asked if I could go to London 'to run a webinar'. 'Could I not run it from Glasgow?', I asked. 'Oh, do you think that would work?' came the reply. I'm pleased to say it did!

But these attitudes persist throughout business and they hold us back. Many businesses experienced a sudden jolt into a more modern way of working when the COVID-19 lockdown came into force. To their credit, some quickly adapted and got to grips with Zoom meetings, Microsoft Teams, Google Meet and all the rest.

There are some obvious advantages. No more time and money spent travelling; less impact on our environment; improved accessibility for people with issues around physically getting to a particular place for a particular time. When we start looking at diversity and representation throughout our businesses, these things matter.

But consider the small business. The start-up. The sole trade guitar teacher, Cognitive Behavioural Therapist or yoga teacher. Many businesses of that nature have a catchment area of a few miles radius around their physical location – the studio, counselling rooms or whatever. By embracing remote working, they are now able to deliver their services to anyone who wants them, anywhere in the world. It helps the business scale up, positions it for export and can improve profit margins.

There are a few steps you can take to get the most out of this form of working. I've seen some business owners where that seems to mean an expensive haircut, a backdrop of a beautiful beach and remembering to actually get dressed instead of sitting in pyjamas when joining a Zoom call. For me, there are a few more serious things to consider.

The first is that lots of people use the word 'webinar' when they mean any form of remote interaction. It reminds me of when my Mum used to say 'Hoover' when she meant any form of vacuum cleaner. Webinars, live streams and video conferences are all different and you should take care to choose the most appropriate delivery method for your business and your audience, and this will dictate the system that you use.

Webinars.

Serious, proper old school. Webinars have been around for decades and have their roots in education. The first webinar didn't have video. You couldn't see anyone, it was all just audio. But there's always someone in charge, often a PowerPoint slide deck to go through and some interaction with the audience. They are often there to learn, rather than to be entertained. Webinars can be live or pre-recorded and can work as a free marketing activity to raise awareness of your products and services, or as a direct revenue generation exercise for a specific audience. Popular webinar platforms include Adobe Connect, WebEx by Cisco, GoToMeeting and GoToWebinar.

Live streams.

As technology has developed with increasing broadband speeds, and in a world where so many of us have a smartphone in our pocket etc., a new wave of remote communication has emerged with emphasis on entertainment and less interaction. Joe Wicks doing his daily PE classes on YouTube is one example. A local football team showing live video of its matches is another. Or a business doing quick behind-the-scenes tours on Facebook Live. Some of these have extremely high production values – multiple cameras, high quality sound, custom graphics etc. Others are no more than one member of the team talking into their smartphone. However you do it, the trick is to remember that all of this is an extension of your brand. You'll be judged on the quality of content you produce. So, by all means, jump on and have a go, but if you've no idea what to say and come across as amateurish, you won't do your business any favours.

Many businesses make the mistake of attempting to replicate their entire business when they look to move to remote delivery. This frustrates them and they sometimes write the whole thing off because there are aspects of what they do that can't be delivered online. I'd suggest a more considered approach. Look at all your products and services, your entire customer base and ask if there are elements of what you do that could be adapted to remote delivery. And then consider whether a webinar, live stream, video conference, or even just a pre-recorded video would work best. Musicians will never replicate the experience of attending a concert at an amazing venue in person, with a live stream from their living room. And they might end up disappointed if they tried to charge the same admission fee for the live stream as they would for a ticket to the full show.

Try to see this way of working as a separate product. It's not a 'poor second best' option while we wait for things to get back to normal. It's different. It has some advantages, some disadvantages but it can give your business an exciting, other dimension.

Video conferences.

If you've ever had a WhatsApp video call with your friends, then you've experienced a video conference. These differ from a webinar because there's no-one 'in charge'. There's no link to access the session and everyone is equal. We can all see and hear each other. No-one 'decides' who gets to speak, as is often the case with a webinar. Video conferences are more intimate. They work best with smaller groups of participants who probably know each other already.

Skype, Facebook Messenger, and Apple Facetime are all examples of video conferencing platforms.

So, how come it's all so confusing?

Because the technology is developing extremely quickly and all the platforms want to be the one all of us use for everyone. Smartphones and improved broadband speeds mean the feature sets are all starting to merge. So Zoom can be used for webinar delivery, but it looks and feels like a video conferencing app. Facebook Messenger is a video conferencing app but if you share your screen you could run the session similar to a webinar. Google has a video calling tool called Google Meet which was originally intended for enterprise level business use, but they'd be perfectly happy if you use it for your family quiz night too.

Don't let yourself get caught up in it all. Think about your business and your audience and what's right for them. Where are they just now? For example, if you've built a following on Facebook, it's asking a lot of your audience to sign up via email to receive a link and password to download and set-up a webinar platform so they can watch your free training workshop on Friday evening. Much easier if you deliver it through Facebook Live, because they are there already. But if I'm a counselling patient and you tell me I can't attend my session in person next week because your office is closed then I might be perfectly happy to take time setting up Google Meet because I trust the end to end encryption and I know that what we discuss in our session will be so beneficial to me. A captive audience who already knows you will be prepared to go to more effort than the general public you're hoping to 'catch' as they browse their social network of choice.

In practice, and having run sessions like these over the last ten years or so, it's likely many businesses will develop something of a 'toolkit' for remote working. Sometimes it'll be a video conferencing call to discuss a project or for an initial 'briefing'; maybe a live stream to run a 'taster' session in the hope it attracts a large, general public audience, some of whom become paid-for clients; as well as perhaps some webinar delivery for groups who have registered in advance and paid for some in-depth training. You could also add some pre-recorded video too. I often meet businesses who start thinking about all this and decide to reject webinars, live streams and video conferences and ultimately decide to simply start creating more videos for their business. And that's no bad thing.

There's no 'silver bullet' that does it all and no shortcut to success. But now is the time to start thinking about how you could embrace this area of business because we're likely to see much more of it going forward. You'll likely end up using a hybrid of several platforms and delivery methods. A good first step, if you haven't already done so, is to attend some sessions delivered by others simply as a guest. Watch the live music stream, or join the free webinar your favourite mindfulness coach is delivering. You'll learn a lot by watching others before going live yourself. Remember to be very careful with security, especially if you are sharing links to anything you're doing across social media.

Be sure to read our later chapter about cyber-security and 'Zoom Bombing' – a serious criminal offence with terrible repercussions for the people on the receiving end; and a terrible thing for your brand to be associated with.

But don't be afraid to have a go, and remember that even through webcams and screens , seeing another's face can make for a powerful connection. It's a basic human need and we are programmed to feel more at ease when we can see the face of the person we are speaking to. Look for opportunities to make this happen in your business and don't let the fear of 'going live', or indeed the technology, put you off.

Lastly, just to say that if you ever see Gary on the other end of a Zoom call, please be aware he DOESN'T actually look like that in real-life and his office is never that tidy. He's not just using a fake virtual background, he's also using the 'touch up my appearance' feature too! #JustSaying.

!GeekAlert

People of a certain age (us) grew up with mass media broadcasting AT us. When I (Colin) was a kid dreaming of being on the radio[56], it was beyond my wildest dreams that I could take something I wanted to say and share it with potentially anyone, anywhere in the world, from wherever I choose. If the possibilities presented by where we have ended up don't excite you, they should.

For live streaming, you should check out OBS Studio (https://bit.ly/etsbook-obs) – free software that helps deliver a professional output using multiple cameras and graphics, while also giving you more control over the sound. It's what many of the professional online gamers use and is well worth a look. ReStream.IO is another nice service, enabling you to live stream to multiple platforms at once without too much technical know-how.

For webinars, GoToMeeting.com is a system which Gary's been using for years to deliver online learning to the students on his Digital Diploma course, and we

---

[56] Gary didn't dream of being on the radio. He dreamt of being Maverick from Top Gun.

both use it fairly extensively to deliver online public sector training (to anywhere between ten and 100 attendees). It's not free, and doesn't have all the bells and whistles some people might like, but it's reliable, simple to use, and tends not to attract some of the malicious intent that Zoom gets.

As for kit, the Rode NT-USB is our microphone of choice for webinars and live streams, and we'd also recommend you buy a dedicated webcam too (any of the logitech HD web cams will do a fine job).

Our final top tip when it comes to webinar delivery is make sure you've got a dual monitor setup. Makes life much easier, allowing you to have one 'live screen' for your audience, and one 'private screen' where you setup slides, read the comments, prepare web pages etc. Trust me, once you go to a two-screen setup, you won't go back!

CHAPTER IN A TWEET

These days, every business is a broadcaster. Whether it's direct from your phone, or a big production with multiple cameras and graphics, it's time to explore live streaming and webinars. Facebook Live with OBS Studio is a good place to start. It needn't be expensive.

08

Paid social media

(and why most businesses do it wrong)

Colin (with some geeky additions from Gary)

Smart businesses recognise that paid social media is here to stay and an important, regular part of the strategy. The laser-focussed targeting options alone mean, when it is done correctly, it can be an extremely powerful and productive activity.

All too often we see businesses doing it wrong and wasting their money when it comes to paid ads.

Some see paying as a desperate last resort and something they do while full of resentment. They remember the early days of Facebook, where if you had 1,000 likes on your page, you could reasonably expect the best part of 1,000 people to see your next post. You will likely get nowhere near that now.

So, businesses tend to do the 'fun' social content day to day quite well, getting decent reach but then at some point they try to sell something and inevitably the reach for that post declines significantly, to the point where it serves very little purpose and certainly doesn't deliver the hoped for return. And so at that point, the business decides to invest some money and pay to force that poorly performing post into the news feed of an often fairly large and general audience which gives them a false, temporary comfort that a least a few thousand people are now guaranteed to see whatever it was they were trying to say. This, of course, is short lived because although the reach improves and people see the sales message, it's still a boring, poor quality post that no-one wants in their news feed, and it still doesn't provide the hoped for result, and now the business is £30 down.

The trick then, is to pay to boost or promote a post which has already performed well, as an organic piece of social media content. Something you've said that got a good result. If you put some budget behind THAT, carefully targeting it at a small, but highly tailored and desirable audience, you have a much better chance of getting the result you want. Social media advertising is about balancing the 'sales' bit of what you are trying to say (e.g. tickets are on sale now for the workshop we are running next Friday) with some sort of fun, interesting or 'social' piece of content. Move away from this big division between mindless 'fun' stuff and 'sales' material and blur the lines. The fun should still meet some sort of wider business objectives. And the posts promoting services and products should still be funny, interesting or useful in some ways. There's an art to it and it's something you should practice.

Another common error is chasing the biggest audience possible, with one very generic ad that fails to really connect with anyone. Maybe you do genuinely have a product that the entire population would want to buy. You're ambitious and you have a universal product. Good for you. But you wouldn't sell it the same way to everyone. And let's look at this word 'audience'. There is no 'audience'. Instead, there are millions of people. Different people. With a huge variety of attitudes, dialects, needs and aspirations. They all have different buttons that need to be pushed! And you can't treat them all the same in one ad. It needs to be tailored.

You're a consumer – what ads do you appreciate?

A great way to see both good and bad examples of paid social media content is to browse your own feeds. As a Facebook, LinkedIn or Twitter user, you'll be just as much a target as anyone.

Try this: Next time you see a Facebook ad (it's usually the second thing in your feed when you login!) click on the three wee dots to the top right of the post, and select 'Why am I seeing this ad?'.

If it tells you that you're seeing the ad because the company in question is trying to reach people in the UK between the ages of 16 to 84, and there's no other targeting criteria, then that company has way more money than sense.

What message does any business have that is suitable for everyone in the UK regardless of age, location, gender, etc.? They don't. If you use Facebook to advertise to millions of people – congratulations, you're a spammer. At best I'll ignore you. At worst, I'll block or report you. In any case, it's not a good reflection of your brand.

Advertising, by its nature, is not something people look forward to seeing. We now live in a world where we 'pause' the ads on the TV and then zoom over them after we've made a cuppa. We install ad-blockers on our computers to minimise the annoyance of commercial, irrelevant messages on our screens. We even avoid things like Google Ads, heading instead straight for the 'organic results' because we know that people have simply paid to be there.

Instead, if the next Facebook ad tells you that you've been targeted because you're 35-45, live in the Aberdeen area, have an interest in small business, and have already been on that company's website, then they've done a pretty good job at being selective about who they've targeted.

Paid ads example

So take, for example, a bicycle shop. They have one advert aimed at young parents buying a toddler his or her first bicycle. The words used in the ad, and the picture they've chosen to accompany it, should reflect the stage in life the parents are at and the bicycle they are likely to end up buying.

And then a different ad aimed at cycling enthusiasts in their 60s, maybe looking at spending more time cycling in their retirement and with different concerns and of course, very different bicycles! So you absolutely can 'talk to the world' if you really want to, but you shouldn't do it in a 'one size fits all' manner. Split it up, segment the audience, and promote specific products, to specific people, in a specific way.

The businesses achieving the most from paid ads take it even further, creating different graphics to better resonate with specific people based on where they are. So a picture of your amazing electric bike with a view of the Queensferry Crossing in the background would make an ideal image for your 'Edinburgh people' advert. Not so much your Glasgow ad. Tailor every aspect of the advert's content and think about what would resonate with the target audience seeing it. What would they actually 'like' to see in their feed that day? It's usually not an advert, so go out of your way to make it look like anything but one.

The beauty of social media advertising is that it is accessible. The pricing structure is such that almost any business can at least try it. Experiment with it, have a go and learn from it.

The aim is to get to the point where you know, for example, that for every £50 you spend on promoted posts, you achieve a clear return on your investment. Once you understand the numbers, you can choose to scale up (or down), achieving equivalent results. Rather than seeing it all as a last ditch act of desperation to try and get a sale, we hope you begin to see it as an ongoing opportunity.

!GeekAlert

Did you know you can easily see all the adverts any business is currently running on Facebook?

Take a look at the Facebook Ad Library -
https://bit.ly/etsbook-facebookads

In an attempt to make Facebook more transparent (and to try and avoid further government scrutiny) they recently made available for public viewing every 'live' advert being run by any organisation on both Facebook and Instagram.

The result is a free tool that can really help with your own ads. Take a look at what your competitors are doing, and see what products and services others in your industry are actually putting their money behind. Or just use it to gain inspiration from bigger brands to see 'how' they do their advertising in terms of tone, images, and call to actions.

It won't show you 'who' other businesses are targeting with their ads, but it does give you a real insight into how other businesses are using it. It's well worth a visit.

Taking things further

Creating niche audiences for your adverts as described above is just the tip of the iceberg when it comes to strategic use of paid advertising on social media. You can also do some pretty amazing (advanced) things with existing data.

If you have a customer mailing list that you've been building (following GDPR guidelines) then you'll likely be able to use it to build a 'custom audience'. The ability to show a promoted post to your existing customers as the platform tries to 'match' your data with theirs. Regardless of whether your customers already follow you on these platforms, you can still reach them effectively.

Facebook call them 'Custom Audiences', on LinkedIn they are 'Matched Audiences' and on Twitter it's 'Tailored Audiences', but essentially they all facilitate the same thing. These audiences can be built not just from email lists (or indeed, any data list which can be imported), but also from website traffic, allowing you to present adverts to people who have already shown an interest in the topic by visiting specific pages of your website. Or perhaps create a custom audience based just on people who already 'engage' with you, as they'll be the most likely to do the same again.

Finally you could consider 'Look-a-like' audiences – a powerful feature which allows you to build an audience based on people who are 'just like' your existing customers or like the people who already follow you. The premise here being that if you're looking to get people to buy from you, then target the people 'just like' the people who have already bought from you. Those with similar traits, interests and values – all the things Facebook (and the others) know about all their users. With my business hat on – seriously powerful stuff. With my consumer hat – terrifying.

Want more followers? Buy them!

The 'paid side' of social media isn't just about adverts. A simple strategy we've seen employed many times with good results, especially for smaller and start-up businesses, is to increase follower numbers by simply buying them! Most of the social networks now allow you to create 'follower campaigns', whereby you pay not to advertise a particular post, but to have your profile as a whole suggested as a suitable business the viewer might like to follow.

That might sound like a contradiction to earlier advice, but to make this work, the same principles apply. Pay to reach the right people, those who you genuinely believe would want to follow you, but just haven't yet found you.

Don't spam the world and beg for followers who won't go on and engage with your content. Instead, carefully target the right audiences, those who you believe are a good fit for your organisation. They could be local to your shop, or parents of children of a particular age, or senior marketing executives working in the city. The advertising capabilities found within the platforms allow detailed and accurate targeting of your preferred audience, so why not pay to introduce yourself to them, and (assuming you do this well) watch those numbers grow.

Even just experimenting with a small budget at the start to increase your numbers, could save months of effort trying to grow them organically; just make sure you have some excellent content - already posted from your profile - ready for them to see when they come to check you out

Stop talking to the world

No matter how you choose to utilise the advertising features of social media, or how you decide to build your paid audiences, remember to focus not on the many, but on the few. The people that you truly believe will want to see what you're pushing into their feeds.

Our mantra at the workshops is:

> **66** Niche content for niche audiences **99**

Stop talking to the world. The world doesn't care. Think carefully about who you know will care – that's who it is worth paying to reach. Get it right, and paid advertising can deliver a significant return on investment. Get it wrong, and you've wasted their time, and your money.

CHAPTER IN A TWEET

Paid advertising shouldn't be something you grudgingly resort to in order to reach a bigger audience. It should be a key part of your social strategy. Don't make the mistake of chasing big numbers and looking like a spammer. Focus on niche content for niche audiences.

09

Social customer service

(and our 'famous' 3 B's)

Gary

In the connected world we live in, our customers

SHARE

everything. (Colin shouted this earlier in Chapter 2, so I feel the need to do the same).

Sometimes there's a big 'share' button to click on, but often it's less formal with social media simply being the natural place to share stories. Good stories, bad stories, good customer service, bad customer service, things you like and things you don't. What was once a 'You'll never guess what Company ABC did to me today....' story in the pub (or the playground, or at the coffee machine) told to just a few selected drinking buddies (or school pals or office colleagues) is happening today, but online, and to an audience that's potentially global.

When was the last time you received good customer service? If I asked you to name a company which impressed you with their response when something went wrong, I'm guessing you'd have a brief think, and then provide one or two names to me. If I asked you to tell me about bad customer service you've experienced, I bet you'd have a few more names rolling off your tongue pretty quickly.

There are essentially two reasons behind this: the first is that as human beings we tend to dwell on the negative. Suffice to say that as consumers we remember the bad, far more than the good – we're evolutionarily programmed to think like that.

The second reason is simply that poor customer service happens more frequently. As businesses, we're often not as good at customer service as we should be. Some organisations are terrible at it. Remember that customer service isn't just about dealing with complaints, and handling angry customers with a bee in their bonnet[57], it's simply the process of providing SERVICE to a customer. You know – that thing they rightly expect.

---

[57] I've never actually had a bee in my bonnet, but then again, I've never had a bonnet – assuming the phrase doesn't relate to my car.

That thing they are essentially paying for, and that thing which ultimately allows you to remind customers how good you are, how much you care, and how much you value their custom.

The examples you thought of – those companies which took you no time to remember – are probably in your mind due to their service flaws, their rude treatment of you, their terrible attitudes, and their lack of empathy and care. I bet I could guess some of the names you're thinking of. I won't (for obvious legal reasons) name them but I'm sure I could. Especially, the bigger companies, including certain utilities, communications and public transport giants. There are a few usual suspects, and when we ask the question (as we often do) in our workshops, the same names crop up time and time again. Yes, they are easy targets, and with a high volume of customers comes the risk of increased customer complaints, but again, I stress – providing good customer service isn't just about resolving complaints, it's about valuing your customer, and because these companies didn't, I'm guessing you told a few people exactly that!

The good companies, those few and far between examples, the ones you had to really think about but still only came up with just a couple of names, they were remembered for the right reasons. They likely impressed you, and I'm guessing (given you can even recall what happened) that they exceeded your expectations. They might have even 'wowed you', and just as you're thinking about them now, you probably told a few people of your delight at the time.

Customer service is the new marketing

There's no hiding bad customer service. It's out there, visible for everyone to see because your customers are making it so. As online customer service expert Jay Baer wonderfully puts it:

66 Customer service is now a spectator sport. **99**

The world is watching, not just the question, concern or complaint in the first place, but your response (or lack of it) too, and how you deal with it (or don't) from that point on.

Do you look like a company that cares and values conversations (even the difficult ones) with customers, or do you look like a 'cut n paste' company, playing it by the rulebook, doing what you can to avoid the 'right thing', at odds with your customer's views, providing 'politician-like' responses which lack any form of humanity, empathy or customer care.

Most are somewhere in the middle. Most think they deliver good (or even exceptional) customer service, but their customers argue otherwise. Most are remembered for the poor service, or (maybe worse?) aren't remembered at all.

Years ago (in the early days of running our Embrace The Space workshops) we would often ask business owners why they weren't yet active on social media. (Many attending back then had yet to be convinced to make the leap). An all too common response was, 'Because they might say bad things about us'. Thankfully, this attitude is one we experience less and less, but it still exists, particularly in certain sectors – public sector organisations and local authorities being typical offenders!

If you're worried about customers saying bad things, then it's probably because they already are. And if this is the case, then they're almost certainly saying them across their social media channels. And if you're not on those same platforms then you're giving them the freedom to say what they want, unfiltered, uncorrected, and without an opportunity to put forward the other side of the story. Businesses aren't judged only by the comments lodged against them, but by their response as well, and not being on social media equals no response.

Bad stuff happens. Even to the best companies. You might occasionally mess up, say the wrong thing, or disgruntle one or more customers. They might feel so upset that they take to their online soap-boxes such as Twitter, Trip Advisor and Trust-a-Trader[58], and it might (most probably will) give you and your reputation a dent. But it's dealing with these situations appropriately, resolving the problem, and meeting (if not exceeding) customer expectations in how you respond, that has lasting impact.

---

[58] Note that not all review sites begin with the letter T.

*Fictional Case Study (honest)

You might be a local hotel owner in Ayrshire who installs an automatic car park penalty system, designed to fine drivers parking on your grounds who are not actually using your facilities (and thereby reducing the parking spaces for legitimate customers). This might backfire, resulting in actual paying customers receiving £100 demand letters (because they didn't know they had to enter their registration number at the terminal in reception). This might lead to Facebook threads from angry locals expressing how outraged they are, with 100s of comments added in as others support their friends, with hints at boycotting the hotel, letters going to the press and @ tagging of local politicians. You might realise you are at fault, apologise, respond on Facebook to every aggrieved customer, and endeavour to make things right. Or you might stick to your guns, and tell the locals it's essentially their fault for not seeing the new parking signs. You might claim that you can't issue refunds and blame it on the car parking company that you've employed. You might hide behind your hotel manager (who's now getting serious grief on Facebook because she tried to help by responding personally to everyone via her own profile). You might stick your head in the sand and hope it all goes away. It might not. You now might be wondering why so few of the locals dine with you anymore. But at least you didn't back down. They were in the wrong after all.

Bloody moaning customers, eh!

Reply to feedback good AND bad

Again, another reminder that customer service isn't just responding to the bad, it's responding full stop.

One of my big bug bears (I have many!) is companies which pander to negative feedback but which disregard anyone saying positive things. Let's all provide extra special service to the people complaining (sometimes without merit) and completely ignore those customers going out of their way to say nice things, recommend you to others, or generally sing your praises.

I'm not saying ignore the bad, and only respond to the good. Of course we need to engage our detractors, but not at the expense of those who also deserve our attention. It's easy for people to rant and moan, it happens all the time. But they are (for most good companies) in the minority. The silent majority are happy customers, few of whom go to the bother of trying to big us up on social media, but often when they do, it passes without even a 'thank you'.

Positive word of mouth is, and always has been, a powerful marketing tool for your business. Negative word of mouth even more so but usually with significant detrimental effect. Social media is 'Word of Mouth on Steroids' (unsure who first coined the phrase), with people not just telling a few others about your business, but potentially telling the world.

I'd like to share with you our famous '3 Bs' customer service strategy. Designed for today's modern connected world:

Be Nice
Be Great
Be Remembered

At NSDesign I try to embed these into every customer engagement we have – I even stuck them up on the wall in huge vinyl letters to remind everyone in the team (not just the customer facing staff) how important each of these 3 Bs are.

Be Nice

It's not rocket science. Above all else – be nice to customers. Genuinely be nice. Not fake nice, not nice to their face but griping about them behind their back. Nice, polite, respectful, professional, treated in a way that you'd want to be treated yourself. Saying sorry when required, and actually meaning it. The irony is that so many organisations hire customer facing staff who genuinely don't ever want to deal with a customer. They won't be nice. They won't respond personally. They'll cut-n-paste, hide behind the brand, quote the rules, and never sign off with their name. Nice shows you care. Nice shows you value customers. Nice is the essence of customer service. If you can't be nice, bring in others who can. Or just stop now. The ONE thing you need in business is a customer. Everything else comes second to that – so start with the simplest of our 3 B's and take it from there.

Being nice on social media isn't difficult. It starts with making sure you acknowledge and respond to everything said to you. If someone tags you in, you respond. Being nice is being conversational – not answering with just a 'yes' or a 'no'. You don't need to write an essay, but a short personal response, which opens the door to further conversation, is a nice way to talk to someone. It's also often the way to further business opportunities. Seriously, why wouldn't you want to keep talking to customers? Conversation builds trust, and trust builds rapport. As a big telecoms company used to say in their jingle – "It's good to talk".

Be Great

Let's be honest – we can't always 'be the best'. It's impossible. We can try, but others might do it better. So don't beat yourself up about not being number one all the time. That said, there's arguably always room to improve. We can all up our game and strive for great. Being great means being better than average, better than good. It means exceeding customer expectations, and having them impressed at the effort you've demonstrated.

A great response to a customer complaining on Twitter about a late train, is to offer an explanation beyond 'because the points on the line have failed'. A great response is to apologise for the inconvenience (the 'be nice' part), tell them about the points failure (the customer expectation part), and then to suggest an alternative route home, giving specific helpful details, having done the research for them (the 'be great' part). Sure, they're still angry at the inconvenience but in terms of your customer service, it will be harder for them to say it's not been great.

Go out your way to be great. Help the customer, and then help them some more. If they ask for your customer telephone number, don't just tell them, but ask if you can call them back. If they ask for help on Facebook, don't tell them, 'Sorry, we don't provide support here, please use our online form', just hurry up and help them, or worst case (if they really MUST use your annoying online form), submit it on their behalf, and follow up with them on Facebook directly when there's an update. If there are hoops to be jumped through, YOU jump through them. Be great!!

Be Remembered

Get the first two Bs right, and you automatically ace the third. Get the first two wrong, and you still get to be remembered, but for all the wrong reasons. And while in the real world, today's news is tomorrow's chip paper (which I don't actually believe, especially as the chip shops no longer use newspapers to wrap our chips in), the internet's memory is like an elephant – it never forgets. (I'm hoping that such a random phrase means we bag Google top spot for it for many years to come!).

That 5-star review on your Google ratings makes a difference. That 1-star review even more so.

CHAPTER IN A TWEET

It's easy to leave a lasting impression with people on social media. Follow the 3 B's of customer service:
> Be nice.
> Be great.
> Be remembered.
Exceed customer expectations with meaningful, personal, helpful responses and you'll be remembered for all the right reasons.

#TrainerLife

Sleeping satellites

Being the intrepid social media trainers we are, there are certain essential tools that we should never be without.

For example: an infra-red clicker for navigating our way seamlessly through our slide presentations. A laptop. The ubiquitous smartphone. (Mine's a Google Pixel, Gary is an iPhone man). On occasion we will carry a set of speakers to make sure audio from our hilarious viral videos can be heard in large training rooms. Sometimes I'll bring a packed lunch. Gary never leaves home without his 'Slippery When Wet' CD.

But above all, the main essential for guys like us is a broadband connection. We love a superfast Ethernet plug-in; we'll take wifi, and in an absolute emergency, because we're so resourceful, we'll even tether up to a 4G mobile phone connection. We like to think we've experienced it all.

Rewind a few years and we were partnering with another organisation to deliver a three day digital festival to small businesses. We had three days packed with amazing speakers and great businesses, some of whom told us it was the best business event they'd ever been to.

The problem was the venue. It was a cracking hotel with a beautiful event space. But it was in a very rural setting, with a patchy mobile phone signal and broadband that couldn't be relied upon to deal with the number of tech savvy businesses we were planning to put in the room.

Thankfully, they'd had the decency to tell us ahead of time. However, we were further complicating matters by insisting our entire event would be live streamed.....and this is back in a time before Facebook Live and even YouTube Live. In fact, we reckon we might have been the first large business conference in the country to live stream!

So the decision was made that we had to, somehow, upgrade the hotel wifi, for three days, without blowing our budget (which was already stretched because we had attracted some extremely high calibre speakers). Several weeks before show time, one of us (neither of us will admit to it now) had the idea of using a new technology called 'satellite broadband'. On the face of it, it looked like the perfect solution. Specially designed for rural situations, very flexible and easy to install, discreet, reliable, and crucially, capable of speeds of up to 20MBPS with up to 100 simultaneous users. If nothing else, we could use that for the attendees and that would mean the hotel wifi would be dedicated for us to run the live stream from. Perfect.

Actually, not perfect.

Day one arrived and the gurus from 'Satellite Broadbands R Us' (that wasn't their name) pitched up and set up their kit. This involved a flimsy looking satellite dish on a tripod in the car park, some CAT-5 cable through an open window to a router stuck to what looked like a microphone stand with some gaffer tape.

The first hint that something might be wrong (apart from the rather patched-together look of it all) was that our friendly satellite broadband installation team......well, let's just say they weren't exactly advocates for their product. I'm sure I overheard some negative mutterings as one of the team tried to connect with the base station.

Sometime later, the network was up and we eagerly logged on not expecting anything blazing fast of course but the 'Better the Devil you know' video without buffering would have been nice.

Gary loads up YouTube from the main room. I wander to the bar area and do the same.

I wait.

He waits.

Gary refreshes.

I refresh.

Still nothing.

We try Google.com

No logo.

Still no logo.

Back to YouTube.

Suddenly, Gary shouts: 'I've got it, I've got something'.

The BBC News webpage had finally loaded.

Now, I've given up on 'Better the Devil you know' and I'm making do with 'Never too late' (the irony).

I skip the five second ad and the video starts to play.

Maybe this satellite broadband thing could catch on after all.

Maybe not.

Kylie gets halfway through the first verse and starts buffering. (Never thought I'd write that sentence).

Out of the corner of my eye, I catch sight of satellite broadband installer man pacing around nervously.

'I've got on but it's buffering mate. It's really slow,' I say, hoping maybe there's a setting that can be tweaked or a wee guy in a van outside that could be shouted at to pedal a bit harder.

Satellite broadband bloke looks me right in the eye as he points towards Gary in the main room and says, 'Aye, I know but mind he's on it as well.'

I bit my lip, went back in and broke the news to Gary. Together, we then experienced mild convulsions before composing ourselves.

In fairness, after this rather shaky start, the satellite broadband crew went over and above what we'd asked for, and what we were paying for, and set us up with the absolute mother of all satellite broadband setups which ensured that we did indeed successfully live stream three nights worth of events and keep 100 or so social media enthusiasts happy in the room. It did end up taking three satellite dishes in the car park, around 400m of cable, two full rolls of gaffer tape and one of Gary's spare network routers[59], but we got there. We always do!

Colin

---

[59] You'll maybe not be surprised to hear that uber-geek Gary carries equipment in the boot of his car which rivals a BT broadband engineer – 'just in case' apparently!

10

Ratings, reviews and recommendations

(and encouraging your customers to do your marketing for you)

Gary

Consumers today are lazy. Don't take it personally – I include myself in that broad sweeping statement. We use things like ratings, reviews and recommendations (a possible next book – 'The 3 R's') to make buying decisions.

The products that usually sell the best on Amazon are the ones which rise to the top when you order the category by Customer Review. Yes, brand loyalty and price point still play important roles, but for some things, the one that everyone else loves, is the one that I'll love too!

FOMO – fear of missing out. My pals all like it, I'll like it too. The world seems to be watching this video, so I'll watch it too. Everyone seems to rate this hotel highly on TripAdvisor, it 'must' be good and I want to go too. Rightly or wrongly, if customers make their decisions based on what other people say, then as businesses we need to get more people saying more of the right things.

And what they say counts. After all, in today's sceptical world, first time customers don't trust you. Again, don't take it personally, they don't trust me either! They don't know me, haven't met me, never experienced our products and services, and so there's a natural bias to be sceptical until proven otherwise. The things I say on the website are potentially all lies: 'Of course you say you're the best – you're trying to sell me something'. Of course you'll tell me about your latest '100% customer satisfaction rating', as if you'd tell me anything else.

A 2018 report from EConsultancy found that:

> **66** 58% of adults don't trust a brand until they have seen 'real world proof' that it has kept its promises.[60] **99**

Personally, I'm surprised it wasn't more. Trust has to be earned, and experienced. Trust comes over time. And if you make the assumption that somebody who's never used you before, doesn't trust you, and therefore is unlikely to buy from you, the realisation dawns that it's a huge challenge to grow a business with new customers at all! Start building trust.

---

[60] https://bit.ly/etsbook-econsultancy

So what do people trust? Other people. Always have, and always will. If you can get other people to tell everyone how good you are, you can dial it down a little. If other people say that our customer service is good, then it's clearly good – straight from the horse's mouth (although we don't have any horses as customers). If our products are an average of 4.9 stars on Amazon, then the stats don't lie do they! (*actually they very often do, especially on shopping review sites where you can buy 100 5-star reviews for £20 if you know where to look, but that's a whole other story for another day).

As we say at the workshops: 'The people become your marketing'. So ask yourself what you're proactively doing right now to try and get more people telling more positive stories about you. How? Well you can start by re-reading the previous chapter, and following the 3 B's, and maybe it will happen naturally. But if not – don't be afraid to just go out and ask people. Ask your customers (obviously the happy ones!) to review you on Facebook, Google, or Trust Pilot. Don't hound them to do it (remember to be nice), but ask and see what happens. And respond with an authentic 'thank you' when they do.

Encouraging user reviews

Third party validation should be core to your marketing strategy. Ask for testimonials for your website (video testimonials especially work a treat), identify the right customers on LinkedIn and request recommendations about your professional services, get all your regulars to review your restaurant on Trip Advisor, or seek comments from your patients about how good a brain surgeon you are on Care Opinion (yes – it does exist).

Which platforms you focus on will depend on which are most relevant to your key audiences, but a few good places to start (for most businesses) include:

Google My Business

We could have listed this 'platform' in Chapter 3, but we'd argue that technically it's not a social media platform, more an extension of the Google search engine. That's not to say it's not hugely important, and influential to your digital strategy. Especially, when it comes to establishing trust quickly. If someone Googles your company name, then included in the results they receive should be your website, links to your various social media platforms etc., and most importantly, information pulled in from 'Google My Business' (GMB). Included in this information are your Google reviews – the volume you've received and your average 5-star rating. If I click on this, it leads me to the actual reviews themselves, where I can read what other people say about you (good and bad), as well as see how you respond.

Google is used by over 90% of the UK internet browsing public. It's the go-to place to quickly find your telephone number, opening hours, directions to your physical premises (if you have them) and get a grasp on whether I should trust you or not. All information found in your GMB profile[61] which you are in full control of. This data is shown on the main Google search page, and also when I look for businesses on Google Maps (becoming increasingly common on mobile phones).

Consider the customer journey: do they just Google you, find you, and buy straight away? Of course they don't. They Google you, and half a dozen others, as they try and work out which business to go with. You looked like a really good web design company, but it's a shame you've only got one 4-star review. The other web design company has 23 reviews, with a 4.8 average. I think I'll call them today. It's not rocket science, and first impressions make a huge difference to establishing trust.

Facebook reviews

Another no-brainer, yet we still see many businesses on Facebook who have opted to turn their reviews off. According to Facebook itself, one in three people use the platform to look for recommendations and reviews. Even when we're not doing this intentionally, we're influenced constantly by what we see while browsing business pages, and more so by what other people say about them (especially if we're 'friends'[62] with them).

---

[61] If you've not yet created a free GMB listing, get it done now! - https://bit.ly/etsbook-gmb
[62] I use that word loosely: it's easy to have lots of 'friends' on social media.

Turn them on (if you haven't already) from the 'Templates and Tabs' section of your Facebook page settings, and start encouraging your customers (especially the happy ones!) to leave you a review.

Technically, Facebook no longer deals in 'reviews', now favouring 'recommendations', but the idea is the same. People can recommend (or not recommend) you by sharing their views about your business directly on your page. Their recommendation also now appears as a post on their own timeline, meaning their friends have a much higher chance of seeing it and being influenced by them (they don't ever need to visit your page to see what others think of you).

Think like the customer. You're looking at a business with no recommendations, or even worse, you realise they've turned that whole section off. What conclusions do you come to? Hardly oozes trust does it? But a business that is willing to actively display what others say about them, which is transparent in how they talk to their customers? That speaks volumes.

TripAdvisor

The Grandfather of review websites – businesses that are impacted by TripAdvisor tend to either love it, or hate it. It depends how it's impacting them! At one end of the spectrum it's a breeding ground of angry customers, determined to ensure the world knows that you provide the 'worst customer service on the planet' (often written by your competitors), and at the other end it's a goldmine of positive sentiment encouraging people to try a hotel which is the 'world's best kept secret' (often written by the hotel owner or their web savvy kids).

Love it or hate it, if you're a hotel, or restaurant, or part of the hospitality industry or leisure industry ('things to do' now being core to TripAdvisor's offerings), then you really cannot afford to ignore it. It's where consumers go to help them make decisions. It helps them decide if you're trustworthy, or if you're family-friendly, or if you allow dogs, or have good wifi. It's jam-packed with things that other people are saying about you, and your next customer likely believes it all more than anything you can say to them.

If you're not there, a huge chunk of your target market won't even realise you exist. Possibly worse is that they do know you exist, are trying to find you on TripAdvisor, and you're not there. Again, what picture might that paint?

Dealing with bad reviews

It might be my rose-tinted view on things, but I genuinely believe good businesses have nothing to fear from the odd bad review. Customers aren't stupid, and so long as it's not ALL bad, most people know that once you remove the extreme reviews, the ones left in the middle ground are usually a fair representation of the organisation.

Good businesses which deliver on their promises, provide great customer service, and which give a damn about doing the right thing, will always come out on top. As detailed in the last chapter, they're unusually remembered for all the right reasons.

But when you ultimately do get that bad review (and it will happen, no matter how great you are, at some point someone will want to have a moan and give you a less than perfect score[63]), then what you don't do is call them out in public, kick off and start a bun fight[64].

Remember that others are judging you on your response, just as much (if not more so) as the actual complaint. Go in all guns blazing, with a he-said, she-said, can you prove it, no you can't approach, then your future customers are now more than a little concerned at how you deal with people, and aren't exactly reassured about how you might treat them should any customer service issues arise later on.

What you should certainly never do is just ignore it (the one exception here being if the customer comment is potential defamation or harassment, in

---

[63] Yes, you know I'm talking to you 'Bruce Fraser', who in 2013 gave us just four stars on Facebook instead of five, and didn't even bother to explain why!

[64] Oops.. er, sorry Bruce. I take it back. We'll try and do better to earn full marks from you next time.

which case quickly skip to Chapter 13, and get some legal advice). Ignoring customers just tends to make them post multiple times to get your (and other people's) attention, and for everyone else watching they see a one-sided conversation, and assume your lack of response amounts to an admission of guilt!

The best advice we always give is actually nice and simple: reply in public, resolve in private.

Give a reply (just one) acknowledging the negative comment or review, and provide a professional, courteous, and (where required) apologetic reply. Some businesses (and their legal advisors) advise against ever saying sorry, warning that's an admission of being at fault, and potentially opening things up to all sorts of legal liabilities. In my opinion, that's misguided. These same companies are the ones that hide behind anonymous email addresses, and whose staff never give out their name. You know the ones I mean.

If someone (anyone) was to phone you today, and begin the conversation with 'I'm phoning to complain about......' then any decent business (and their staff) would immediately reply with the words, 'I'm sorry to hear that, let me take more details and get to the bottom of this'. And that's what we suggest you do online too. Respond in public, and then aim to resolve in private. If they are indeed a customer then you'll already have their email or phone number, so advise them that you'll investigate further, and get back to them directly.

It's in no one's interest to have an open dialogue about what happened, who said what, what the order number was, or what the customer's mother's maiden name is. This is private information, and you have a duty of care to protect the customer's data (even the angry ones).

Also, be aware that getting into a back and forward discussion actually pushes that review out to more people. Remember our previous advice on 'engagement' and how the greater the viewer engagement the greater the reach that content achieves. It's typically the same for reviews; so on Facebook, for example, if you only provide a thread of comments back and forth on the bad reviews, you're pushing them all to the top of the list! Don't do this, and if you must reply more than once, ensure the good reviews get just the same (if not more) attention to help them appear first and more frequently.

While you should always try and take the complaint offline, you cannot always guarantee the customer won't aim to do the opposite – keep it online and public, often coinciding with upping their energy levels, and colourful abuse. Don't bite. You've acknowledged the complaint, and will follow through directly as advised. At this point, anybody following the discussion will now start to see the complainer for who they are, and if you need to (because of foul language, or threatening behaviour) you'd be well within your rights to start editing and/or deleting comments, to protect yourself, your staff, and the rest of the viewing public. Should you need to do this, comment and explain why you've deleted their post, and that you will not accept that sort of behaviour/language. If it turns nasty, learn how to block, report, and if necessary, record the evidence for legal follow up.

But I repeat, good companies have nothing to fear from negative reviews. I've seen so many examples of negative reviews being turned around. With the final word from an initial angry customer being 'thank you'. Follow the earlier 3 B's and all should be good.

Embrace lazy consumers

In today's connected, time short, sceptical world, your customers have more marketing power than you do. People trust other people, especially if they know them (social reinforcement is a huge influencer). The last plumber I hired to fix a leaky tap I found on LinkedIn. Seemed decent, AND my mate Paul had recommended him, so that's who I called.

It's what people do: we're lazy, and we make quick decisions, based on things other people say. Although on a personal note, can I urge some caution to those of you picking brain surgeons based on how many shiny gold stars they have. Maybe just a little more research first?

CHAPTER IN A TWEET

Online ratings and reviews are key to building a trusted first impression in today's digital space, so encourage them at every opportunity. Potential customers believe what others say about you, more than what you say yourself. The people become your marketing – use them!

11

"You should buy this awesome energy drink"

The rise of the social media influencer

(and how to get the most for your money if using one)

Colin

I've worked with a few brands recently which have been enticed by individuals who refer to themselves as social media 'influencers'. Some of them do a good job, but the stereotype is a particularly attractive member of our species, who has amassed a huge (hundreds of thousands or millions) social media following, and now charges companies like yours thousands of pounds for the honour of having them send their followers a few messages about your business.

I'm wary of anyone who refers to themselves as a social media 'influencer'. And some of the businesses I know which have used them, were left disappointed with the return they got for the money they spent.

Here's what can sometimes go wrong and what to do instead.

A different approach to influencers

People who call themselves 'influencers' often do so because they have built large audiences that they now wish to monetise. Some even have an agent who negotiates fees on their behalf. The problem is, this large audience was probably built on content entirely unrelated to your business. Or any business. It could be that the 'influencer' shared pictures of themselves at the gym every day, or looking great in their latest beach wear. Or they regularly shared amazing advice on how to build a business and get rich. Often, the content is 'lifestyle' based and very aspirational. Yes, they have a huge number of followers and a great relationship with them, but those followers might not know much about you and have no desire to have your products and services forced upon them. The influencer does their bit and sends out the messages, but the audience at the other end pass it by, preferring to focus their attention on the genuine, authentic content they were there for in the first place. Done extremely well, there certainly can be exceptions to what I'm talking about here, but I'd certainly urge you to approach anyone in the 'influencer' business with caution.

What can achieve better results is to bypass the self-appointed 'influencer' and focus instead on the next level down. Someone with a following in the thousands or tens of thousands. Someone recognised as influential within their own, very tight niche. A medium-sized fish in a very small pond. An influencer who doesn't recognise themselves as an influencer. And who perhaps hasn't given much thought to whether they can monetise their content. They just get on with things and certainly don't have an agent.

Partnering with these individuals can, I believe, be much more productive. First, the costs shouldn't be as high and their followers can be a lot less fickle. Rather than working from a set price list of fees, such as 'Three Tweets for xxx', you'll be able to negotiate something far more useful and tailored to you and your audience. I prefer the word 'ambassador' to 'influencer'. 'Creator' is another good one, because it suggests the individual is there to work with you to create content that works for you, your audience AND the creator who is sharing it. If I was working with a creator or ambassador, in exchange for a fee, I would expect the individual to perhaps attend an event for my business, or to have some pictures and video which would also go on my own business channels, in addition to theirs. And I would want ongoing activity, over an extended period of time. There needs to be sustained involvement from the 'influencer' or 'ambassador' not just a one off 'hit'. So it might be one month's worth of activity. Some pictures, a personal appearance, some video, a series of posts on their own channels and mine, maybe donating a competition prize I can give away. An ongoing relationship where you dictate the terms, not them or their agent.

These relationships work best if you collaborate on the content the influencer shares. Don't let them create it all – work together. Listen to their expertise as they share knowledge of what they know about their audience and what is likely to appeal to them, but at the same time, you need to speak up and be clear about what you need to get across about your business. Choose your partner carefully and work together and you'll have a good chance of getting the result you want.

A good example of a partnership

I worked recently with a shop that made dance costumes for girls that take part in dance competitions. The shop didn't make great use of social media but the owner recognised that the audience, these young women, were prolific users of the main channels and some had large audiences of their own. She didn't feel comfortable trying to 'sell' to these young people as a business on social media and she didn't think they'd be particularly interested in engaging with her channel, even on a social or fun level. Instead, she got in touch with one of the teenage girls (the daughter of a friend, someone she could reach safely and responsibly) and asked if she would be interested in a commission-based arrangement. So the teenage girl shares posts and content, in the same style as her everyday material but from time to time will mention the shop where she got her dance costume, and perhaps shares a special discount code. This allows the shop owner to measure exactly what impact this relationship is having and what sort of return she is getting for her money. Better still, if no money changes hands and the influencer simply receives free products. What makes the difference is the genuine partnership and collaboration rather than you just doing what the influencer tells you. It has to be authentic and tailored. As word got round about this particular example I'm referring to, other young dancers were approaching the business, asking if they could be involved too. Many had audiences running into the thousands. And so the business was able to build an 'ambassadors' programme, with several customers earning a commission as they worked to bring in more sales via their own social media channels.

Take care dealing with under 18s

We've used young people in this example, and care should be taken when trying to engage people under 18 on social media. In many cases, you simply wouldn't do it, unless you knew them already through your family or other sources. When you do form business relationships with social media users, it's important this is properly declared. The main platforms now allow whoever is posting the content to declare a 'paid partnership' and there's a long list of businesses and influencers who have fallen foul of the authorities (not to mention suffered a backlash from their audiences) because they passed off a paid post as an authentic piece of everyday content.

!GeekAlert

The Advertising Standards Authority makes sure businesses stick to the rules when promoting themselves. They have a great resource to keep you right when it comes to social media promotions and working with influencers. You can access it here:

https://bit.ly/etsbook-asaguide

CHAPTER IN A TWEET

When it comes to finding social media influencers, don't play the numbers game. Think quality first and aim for long standing relationships with 'creators' or 'ambassadors' with a hard won, relevant audience rather than wannabe celebrities promising a short cut.

12

Tone of voice

(and developing your brand personality)

Colin

Should you swear on social media?

At first the question sounds ridiculous – there's no other communication platform where a business would drop an F bomb in front of a customer. Imagine the train company wishing you 'a fu***ng great day' when you call up to ask about their timetable. 99.999% of the time, businesses do not swear in front of customers. And those that do have probably made a monumental mistake they'll apologise for and vow never to repeat.

But social media is different. Authenticity reigns supreme. Your audience, your followers might be 'super-fans', or even friends, if it's possible for a business to have friends. And how many of us can honestly say we never swear in front of our friends?

For many of you reading this, swearing on social media in the name of your business would be a step too far. But our attitudes towards foul language give us valuable insight into how we are perceived, and how we want to be perceived, and helps us start to think about the audience we are speaking to. There's no doubt social media is a less formal place than other business communication platforms. Think about how the platforms have evolved. Twitter began as an SMS short form messaging tool. It was like texting, with a character limit of 140 characters per message. That forced brevity gave rise to the use of 'text speak' and a related etiquette designed to get maximum information and emotion across in as few words as possible. Emojis and GIFs followed, and you can trace the emerging social media 'language' all the way back to the mid-90s and the rise of the first wave of internet message boards and newsgroups.

Businesses communicating on the internet came much later, after Facebook, and the like, had built platforms that huge swathes of the population (fast approaching two billion people) were using. So people were there first. And, no surprise, they communicated the way people like to communicate. Informal, emotional, straight to the point and with little thought for convention. They did what worked and what the community expected.

Then along came business, trying to talk the way business is supposed to talk. 'Award winning', 'robust', 'customer centric' etc. and all the other buzz words you find in the average annual report. We shouldn't be surprised that this doesn't work and yet many businesses still persist with it. This formal, business-speak might still have a place in your office, in your brochure and even on areas of your website, but it's rarely well received on platforms like Facebook, Twitter and Instagram. At worst, it marks you out as a business that doesn't really 'get it'.

Smart businesses figured this out early and developed 'brand values' which would dictate the way they came across. Less formal, down to earth, maybe even friendly and fun. And you can take that to extremes and include that style even in places you wouldn't normally expect to see it, such as email footers and copyright notices at the front of books.

The likes of smoothies giant Innocent, Virgin Trains and Brewdog, provided good examples and were followed by other organisations which invested the time and energy into really understanding their audience. Scotrail, the police, various local authorities, all quickly realised that social media is a game to be played. You have to be part of the community, not an organisation talking 'at' people or talking 'down' to them. You have to literally speak the same language as your audience.

That's easy if you do sell smoothies, or cakes, or you're a well-resourced transport company or local authority telling everyone about the town's Christmas lights switch on. Organisations like that tend to have large audiences that sometimes actually want or need to receive information from them, and they resource their communications to reflect this.

It's all a lot harder if you are a small legal firm, you sell scaffolding to businesses, are a recruitment agency or a plumber. How should you talk on social media?

These simple rules should help.

1. Speak like a human, not an organisation.

Social media is a very personal, one-to-one medium. Stop thinking of yourself as a business broadcasting a message, and concentrate on more intimate one-to-one communications. See people as individuals rather than 'traffic' and audiences.

2. Understand the etiquette.

GIFS and emojis are part and parcel of social media. Everyone uses them, even organisations like HMRC. If you refuse to, you look like you're not really part of the community, and worse, might even be perceived as thinking you are superior to those who do. So loosen up. There might not be emojis, text speak and GIFS in your annual report but there's a strong case for them on your social media platforms.

3. Learn the art of being friendly, but still professional.

There's a fine line and it's a tricky balance. But it can be done. Loosening up doesn't mean you don't care. You should still do your best with spelling and grammar. You can have fun without being flippant about serious issues. Pick another business in a similar sector which seems to be doing well with their social media and see if you can take some inspiration from how they are doing it.

4. Be consistent.

This is especially important if there are several of you actually posting the messages on behalf of your organisation. As individuals, we all have our own preferences and ways of doing things. But business social media channels require a consistent tone of voice. You can't be all down to earth and fun with emojis and text speak on a Monday when Rachel is doing the posts and then serious and formal with some corporate jargon thrown in on a Tuesday when it's Richard's turn. Consider developing a simple 'style guide' document. Something quick and accessible that can get pinned to the wall so you'll see it when you're updating the company's social media channels. Include some specific examples of what's good and what's not; so, for example, would you say 'good morning', 'hello', 'hi' or 'hey everyone!'? Are there some topics you would not ever discuss? Where do you draw the line in terms of humour and attitude? You can never plan for every eventuality and you won't get it right all the time, but going through the process of creating a social media style guide forces you to address some issues, gets everything out in the open and increases the chances of your team all being on the same page and getting it right.

The tone of voice your business uses on its social media channels goes right to the heart of your company culture. What kind of business are you? How do you speak to people? What's your attitude towards customers? And your staff?

Many organisations end up using the launch of their presence on social media as an opportunity to refresh their brand values and to have a good look at their company culture. This informs the tone of voice.

It's much easier for a business to get results from social media if it genuinely is a social organisation. Perhaps it's worth attempting to challenge any old attitudes, and tackle any remaining superiority, sexism and lack of diversity, if any of that is an issue for you.

Become the best organisation you can be, before putting yourself under the social media spotlight.

There's no 'one sizes fits all' when it comes to tone of voice. What works for one organisation won't work for another. It is all about what's appropriate for the audience.

66 Be the colour the rest of your industry forgot. **99**

The above quote by Hugh MacLeod[65] is a powerful one, and one we like to share with our Embrace The Space participants; Gary and I now include it every time we run the course. Sometimes properly embracing social media can bring about a reinvigoration of the entire business. We've seen it in some of our participants at the end of the course. They come in at the start referring to themselves as 'a bit of a dinosaur' and by the end of the day they've reconnected with their customers, properly understood what's unique about themselves and remembered why they got into all this in the first place. They rediscover a love for what they do.

It's an emotional moment and emotion is at the heart of good communication. You'll never communicate with emotion if you don't allow yourself to feel it in the first place: so go on that journey, ask these questions of yourself –

---

[65] Artistic Director at Gapingvoid Culture Design Group – a leading Culture Design™ consultancy.

what do you stand for? What kind of business do you want to be? Why do you do what you do?

Let's close this chapter by returning to the question we started with. Is it OK for your business to swear on social media?

Cara Mackay is the Managing Director of Gillies and Mackay, a 30 year old prestigious timber building company based in Perthshire, Scotland. Gillies and Mackay have a clear vision, which is described by Cara as, 'We make the best fucking sheds in the world'. Cara wrote an infamous article on LinkedIn: 'How To: Fucking Work From Home' which received viral attention for the language she used. However, it was in the comments section of that LinkedIn post that the true colours of 'LinkedIn vs Shed Girl' (as it became known) really came through.

Cara has spoken professionally throughout the UK and internationally about her experience of online vitriol. Her talk deals specifically with the response to this article and others, whereby Cara is attacked for swearing. And especially because she is a woman who is swearing.

I asked Cara what her customers think about her swearing, here's what she had to say:

"My customers don't buy from me because I swear and they don't NOT buy from me because I swear. My customers buy from me because they believe in the same things I do about why I make sheds, the way I make them, the way I sell them and then the way I look after them. My business is a success because of every aspect of who I am, not despite it. When I write something and publish it, I stand by it, I believe in it, and I never apologise for it. (A bit like my sheds). Sometimes I swear, sometimes I don't and that's because swearing for me is an expression – not a gimmick, tactic or trend.

Do I think YOU should swear in YOUR marketing?

No.

Especially if you're asking that question instead of just doing it."

Cara has grown her shed business profit exponentially since becoming Managing Director and has just received further funding to do it again over the course of the next two years. As she leads her family business into its second generation, everyone in her company fully understands what it means to pick a lane, get out of the grey and choose a path. Success is what it means.

We're all fully aware of how much noise is on social media, so when you see something raw, human and relatable it's no wonder that's the kind of content audiences actually engage with.

CHAPTER IN A TWEET

Authenticity reigns supreme on social media. Humanise your brand with a consistent tone of voice and a personality that your audience can relate to. Ensure everyone across your organisation understands how you talk to people, and the brand values you want to convey.

*Time for nostalgia - with some classic case studies

Ok, we're approximately half way through the book, so time for a throwback (as us DJs like to call it!).

Gary likes to tell the world how much he loves Bon Jovi. But he doesn't talk quite so much about how much he also appreciates the music of A-ha, Steps and Little Mix. Anyway, we both love our music and like any good band, we have our own 'Greatest Hits'. These are the social media stories and case studies we used to share in the early days of Embrace The Space. You might say these are the businesses and examples that made our course what it is today. Some of these are still part of our training and some were 'retired' some time ago. But they all contain something we think you can learn from.

The Shower Guys

These were a couple of plumbers from Edinburgh who specialised in bathroom installations and were among the first small businesses to get to grips with regular video content. They kept it really simple and highlighted the quality of their work, zooming in so you could see, for example, how smooth the grouting was, the lengths they'd go to to keep whatever house they were in tidy, and always being sure to have some fun and let their personalities shine through. On one level they were simple 'before and after' clips. But on another they were sophisticated but very authentic marketing videos.

Albions Oven

This is probably my all-time favourite social media story because it's so simple and absolutely focussed on using social media for a crystal clear business objective. The Albion Cafe in Shoreditch, London, was an early user of Twitter and, like many businesses, had to address the question: what exactly should we do with this thing? As we often advise any other business in a similar position, the answer lies in our three rules – Know Your Business, Know Your Audience, Give Them Something They Want To Share. So, Point 1: we sell pies and sausage rolls. Point 2: the audience were office workers wanting a quick bite for lunch. And the 'something' to share? Why not super-serve the most loyal customers by telling them when the food had just come out of the oven. Imagine the scene in the offices in the immediate vicinity of the bakers shop, when the Tweet comes out saying the food is ready and one member of staff sees it and shouts to their colleagues 'that's the sausage rolls ready – who wants one?'. That alone would be worthwhile and might drive increased sales. But does that mean a member of staff at the Albion Cafe has to stop what they're doing to write Tweets every time there's new hot food available? No. And this is the really clever bit. The ovens did the Tweeting. A digital agency across the road from the cafe built a clever piece of kit which meant every time the oven timer went off, a Tweet went out, telling the Cafe's followers what was available and to come and get it! We love the simplicity of this idea. It also highlights the fact that you CAN sell directly on Twitter. If you do it in a way that means something to your audience. Particularly, if that involves real-time information, which Twitter is particularly strong at. I think this has been lost in the last few years as businesses come up with more and more creative and complex ways of promoting themselves. It feels like every business wants 'engagement'. There's nothing wrong with wanting 'sales'. And if you go about it the right way, you might achieve that, with little or no additional work.

> **❝** The idea actually arose from quite a selfish desire.
> They [the web-savy regulars to the bakery] just wanted
> a way to get the freshest baked stuff first. **❞**
> **Albion Manager, David Dedrick**[66]

United Breaks Guitars

'Treat a customer well and they'll tell one other person', goes the famous phrase, 'Treat them badly and they'll tell ten'.

Musician Dave Carroll had a bad experience when he flew United Airlines with his guitar. Long story short, it arrived badly damaged at his destination and a lengthy battle ensued as Dave tried to get the airline to take responsibility for what happened.

The entire saga is now part of customer service folklore and Dave, feeling he was being ignored and fobbed off by United's customer services team turned to YouTube in an effort to get his point across. He wrote a song, detailing his experience and roped a few friends in to star in a low budget but highly creative music video. The end result, 'United Breaks Guitars', uploaded in May 2009 recently passed the 20 MILLION VIEWS barrier on YouTube. It's featured on the mainstream media, led to a book and speaking tour for Dave, and serves as a powerful reminder that social media gives huge power to the individual. One unhappy customer, one bad experience, one issue that previously might have

---

[66] https://bit.ly/etsbook-albionsoven

been swept under the carpet and ignored, can now lead to serious damage to your brand.

You can watch Dave's video here: https://bit.ly/etsbook-unitedbreaksguitars

Four Seasons Hotel, Chicago

Almost every business in the hospitality sector prides itself on 'customer service' and 'attention to detail'. Those are easy things to say on a website or social media biography but what does it actually mean in practice?

This hotel, in the early days of Twitter, used it to do something really clever. And this is something else I feel has been lost as advertising and marketing departments get their teeth into social media, letting creativity run rampant in the quest for new customers and 'engagement' and forgetting their original objective.

This hotel used Twitter purely as a listening tool. Local staff at the reception desk had access to the account (something that's increasingly rare these days as most large chains have social media teams operating centrally) and could monitor Twitter for any mention of their particular hotel. They had the authority to take whatever specific action was required, in order to deliver outstanding customer service to the customer staying with them.

There have been scores of great moments over the years as a result of this strategy, leading to tremendous good will and customers becoming advocates for the brand. You should ask yourself what your business could do by using Twitter or Instagram more as a 'listening tool' and acting on the information you discover.

My favourite story about this particular Four Seasons in Chicago is when the guest arrived ahead of her speech at a major business conference, checked in, and having inspected the bathroom, realised her preferred brand of shampoo was not the brand the hotel made available. Hardly an earth shattering customer service disaster, but, as something of a self-confessed diva, she turned to Twitter, tagged in a few of her friends and wrote words to the effect of 'Look at me, I'm never happy.....in a beautiful hotel and moaning about the lack of 'insert favourite brand of shampoo' in the bathroom'.

I'm not sure she even tagged in the hotel itself. She wasn't complaining. It was a throwaway bit of fun between friends, that just so happened to be public on Twitter.

The front desk reception staff saw the message later that evening as they had various alerts set up for any Tweets from guests or mentions of their specific location. Rather than 'engaging' as so many brands do now, the staff took action. Put a note under the guest's door explaining they'd seen the Tweet and would have that particular brand in her bathroom the next night. The guest was delighted, immediately going back onto Twitter and telling her followers about the hotel's response and what a great place it was.

There's a fine line for businesses here because you wouldn't want customers to feel you were 'stalking' them or eavesdropping on everything. You also have to be careful not to artificially raise expectations to the point where it becomes impossible for the business. What would they have done if she'd complained to her friends that Brad Pitt wasn't in the room to read her a bed-time story?

But done well, and carefully, social media, and Twitter in particular, is a very powerful tool that allows you to see what people are saying about you right now. What you do with that information, of course is up to you. But I think it's worth keeping in mind the opportunity to take action, to turn an experience round, to deliver a 'wow' moment, rather than simply 'engaging'. Much of this requires the business itself to empower local staff, at each specific local site, and we still see many businesses getting this wrong and keeping social media locked down at central HQ.

KLM Surprise

Dutch airline KLM followed a similar path with their #KLMSurprise campaign. If a passenger checked in for their flight and was then stuck at the gate because their flight was delayed, and had Tweeted about how frustrating this was (as fed up travellers often do), the KLM team would find it, look through the individual's Twitter timeline to get a sense of what kind of work they did, why they were travelling and any hobbies or interests they might have, and would then buy them a gift (perhaps a travel pillow, a pair of headphones, a book etc.) from one of the airport shops, track them down and give it to them. Sometimes, the moment the passenger was found and the gift presented was captured on video which KLM later shared through their social media channels.

This activity generated a lot of goodwill towards KLM, encouraged many passengers to follow them on social media and turned what could have been a negative into a positive with people going onto social media and telling all their followers explicitly what a good experience they'd had with KLM, and 'why can't every airline be like this one?'.

Another great example of a business that cares about its customers, using the technology to deliver an enhanced service. That should be the priority for everyone.

13

Social media dangers

(and staying on the right
side of the law)

Colin

Right, I'm rolling my sleeves up now, putting on my 'stern' face and getting ready for:

The dangers

People ask us all the time, 'Can I get sued for something I say on social media?' (you can) and 'Would that be something the police would be interested in?' (maybe) and 'Why did the late magician Paul Daniels block Colin on Twitter?' (try a Google search).

Twitter has been described as a 'cesspit' and we've had more than one participant on our workshops refer to Facebook as 'the Devil's spawn' or 'a necessary evil'. These sorts of quotes always stir up an interesting debate about whether or not social media is a 'force for good' but whatever you think, there's no doubt we are dealing with some powerful tools here and we never shy away from discussing the dark-side of things and how businesses can be negatively impacted.

Use some common sense (and pass it on to your staff if you have any) and it's unlikely you'll cause much upset or fall foul of the law. The advice that follows (which is not professional legal advice by the way, so don't come crawling to us if things go Pete Tong) will give you an idea of some of the risks you might encounter and a basic awareness of how to protect yourself and your business.

The vast majority of business users of social media will never post anything that remotely crosses over into territory that would elicit interest from the police or the courts. The truth is most businesses are far too boring for any of that. And that's the problem. In the pages that follow we'll deal with some extreme situations. But a far more likely risk is that what you say doesn't get noticed at all, doesn't cut through and doesn't meet any of your business objectives. For most, the biggest risk when it comes to social media is that their poor use of it wastes their time. The advice throughout the rest of this book should take care of that. What follows will help you avoid the real nasty stuff.

Defamation

This is an area of civil law. That means you won't get the police at your door but could end up getting sued.

Defamation (slander if it's spoken word and libel for the written word) is an untrue statement that does, or could, have the effect of lowering someone's reputation.

That's a very broad spectrum, but the reality is even being threatened with a defamation action can be disastrous for a business because the costs of hiring lawyers to defend yourself against it can quickly become astronomical.

Where a defamatory statement is made, the original publisher of the statement can be sued, as well as anyone who repeats it or, for example, allows it to be published on a Facebook page, Twitter stream or message board. In addition to that, if it can be demonstrated that the message was written or shared by a member of your staff, using company property, while on the company premises, during business hours, then it might be possible for the business itself to be sued as well as the individual staff members.

So Celebrity A says something defamatory about Celebrity B (calls them a liar, a racist, a cheat, a drunk – there are a multitude of possibilities). Your Sales Director retweets the message along with 5,000 other people. Your Sales Director and your business as a whole, could be included in the legal action raised by Celebrity B. Oh, and to save you the bother of looking it up, business insurance often doesn't include the costs of defending a defamation action.

You don't hear much about defamation actions in the news because the vast majority of claims settle out of court. If you're unlucky enough to become embroiled in one, they are extremely difficult to get out of. In Scotland, there is no 'threshold of seriousness' as there is in England. Libel law in England was recently reformed, and in cases where there is no substantial damage to an individual or their business the case is unlikely to proceed. In Scotland, it is not necessary to show that actual damage or loss of income or earnings has occurred. It is enough simply to show that the statement was made, that it was untrue, and that it could have the effect of lowering someone's reputation. Most of us simply cannot afford the money, or the time, to get into an argument, in court, arguing about what was meant when you referred to an individual as 'a liar' and the finer points of their honesty and the extent of the damage this has caused them. In practice, what often happens is the lawyer would write to you, demanding your statement is removed, that you apologise, promise not to repeat your untrue claims and to pay the wronged party an amount in damages and legal fees, which might be several thousand pounds. If you refuse, it's then up to them to take matters further and to actually lodge proceedings against you, at which point, the costs and the risks rocket.

Faced with this, the majority of cases settle and are never heard in court.

It has been considered defamatory to call someone a liar, a cheat, an alcoholic, a bankrupt, a criminal, a child abuser, an illegitimate child, a racist, incompetent and a great many other things. It is an almost exhaustive list. Remember, it can be anything that is untrue and which could lower an individual or a company's reputation.

There are exceptions. Obviously, if you are able to prove that your original statement was true, then you can use the special defence of 'veritas' or 'truth' — but you would still have to go to court and engage the services of a lawyer in order to do this. Statements made by politicians within the Houses of Parliament cannot be defamatory and this extends to comments made in certain other 'privileged' settings.

Puerile abuse also cannot be defamatory. That of course, does not mean you should engage in it, especially not under your business name, as it is unlikely to do your reputation any good. You are also entitled to give a fair review. So you could say, 'I had a steak in Colin's Restaurant last night and it was horrible, it was cold, the worst steak I've had in my life, and the staff made me feel really unimportant'. You are quite entitled to say that. If you went on to say that the Chef was hungover, that they didn't wash their hands before cooking and that they'd been fired from their previous job in the restaurant down the road (assuming these statements were all untrue) then you would be leaving yourself open to a defamation action.

A defamation claim can be lodged in any jurisdiction where the message was received. So, in the case of social media, if the message was written in Scotland but read or could have been read in England, Ireland, New Zealand, Canada, Germany etc. etc., then the aggrieved party could, if they wished, take action in all of those locations.

A defamation action is expensive and time consuming for everyone involved and judges expect both parties to try to resolve matters before they come to court. If you delete and apologise for any offending message at the earliest opportunity you will save yourself considerable time and money. It's important that you have a process for dealing with complaints and requests to remove offending material and that you are able to action these quickly.

Staff training can help with this. The vast majority have absolutely no desire to get themselves or the organisation into legal trouble and when it is explained to them what defamation involves and the potential consequences, will moderate their own behaviour and stay on the right side of the law.

You should also be aware of what third parties might write on your social media pages, websites, or forums, as you can be held responsible for this if you allow it to remain. Moderate your page, delete and take appropriate action regarding any material that gives you cause for concern. Don't ignore complaints or take down requests.

And don't fall into the trap of believing your business or social media profile is too small for anyone to care. In the eyes of the law, a Twitter account with a handful of followers is treated in exactly the same manner as a national newspaper with a million readers.

Copyright

When a picture is taken, or a graphic or piece of clip-art created, copyright exists automatically and it rests with the creator of the image or piece of work. That means, that if you engage the services of a freelance photographer to take head and shoulders shots of your staff, and you pay their invoice, and start using the images, even then, the copyright is still held by the photographer, and always will be, unless, they agree to handover their rights to the images, or provide you with a licence to use them, in exchange for their invoice being paid.

Don't assume that just because you paid the photographer's invoice that you automatically have the right to use the images anyway you wish, for as long as you want. It doesn't work like that.

Whenever you are engaging the services of an external professional – whether it's a photographer, copywriter, designer, musician, advertising creative etc. – be very clear on the terms of use for the finished work.

Copyright abuse is theft. You cannot visit someone's website, 'right click, save as' or screenshot an image and then use it on your own site or social media. Some photographic studios and licensing organisations have software that trawls the internet, looking for unauthorised use of their work. When it is found, it cross-references the website with a registered office address and sends out a copyright claim and a fine. It's a bit like receiving a fixed penalty notice for driving through a bus lane — but much more expensive.

In my opinion, Google Images is one of the most dangerous places you can look for pictures to use on your website. Many of the pictures you will find are 'scraped' from Google's indexing of the web. It doesn't know for sure which ones are entirely royalty free and available for use, which ones require a credit and a link to the creator, and which ones cannot be used at all. It tries to work this out but it doesn't always get it right. And if you rely on Google, use an image without permission or an appropriate credit and get it wrong, then the fine is on you.

!GeekAlert

If you must use Google to find images to use as your own, at least do the basics. Search for your chosen keywords on the images tab, but make sure that you click on Tools, and set the 'Image Rights' to 'Labelled for Reuse' (choose non-commercial reuse only if you're a not for profit or charity). You'll be disappointed as most of the good images will vanish, but at least what's left will minimise any risk of copyright claims against you!

Safer places to try are www.pexels.com and www.pixabay.com which include large numbers of completely free and unrestricted images to use. Just make sure you double check the details on any specific image you want to use.

We suggest including these as part of your own 'images toolkit' which should also include some pictures you've taken yourself, perhaps some you've paid for from iStockPhoto or Shutterstock and perhaps some from a professional photographer you've hired.

Modern businesses using social media will use images at a vast rate and you need a good collection from a variety of sources. Keep them organised and labelled so that you know which ones you can use and when, and under what circumstances, for example, do they require you to credit the copyright holder.

I know one organisation which kept all their images in one folder and ended up completely unsure which ones they'd taken themselves, which required credits, which they could use forever and which ones needed to be relicensed after one year. The result, of course, was that they couldn't use any of them with confidence which was time consuming and costly, not to mention extremely frustrating.

We've talked about images here but exactly the same applies to music, video and any other creative work. See the section on 'Podcasting' for details of where to access royalty free music for use in podcasts and videos.

Contempt of court

We live in a world where bad things happen and the resulting media coverage and social media discussion makes it very tempting to express your views.

Always remember that as soon as someone is charged with an alleged offence, 'proceedings are active' as far as the law is concerned and this means you cannot say anything which might prejudice the outcome of a trial.

For example, in recent years there have been distressing situations involving a child which have caused great pain in a local community, and quite understandably expressions of horror/disgust etc. on social media. Sometimes, the police will make an arrest and the media will publish details of that individual. Perhaps it's someone in the family or another individual in the community.

What we then sometimes see is people taking to social media making statements such as, 'I knew it was her' or 'He always looked guilty' and 'What kind of person does this?', 'I hope they throw away the key' etc., etc.

All of those statements, if they are made at any point between someone being arrested and charged and the point at which either the case is dismissed or the case completed by way of a verdict, would be guilty of contempt of court.

The penalties for this are severe, and you can, in fact, go straight to prison. Take extreme care, and tell your staff to take extreme care, not to post anything at all that could affect the outcome of a court case or potential course case and don't say anything which implies guilt.

If you are determined that you have to mention the situation at all on your social media, it is best to simply stick entirely to the facts. For example, 'A 46 year old man has been arrested in connection with the death of xxxxxx from xxxxx'. Or, 'a 32 year old woman has been charged with the murder of xxxxx'.

That really is all you can say. And be careful even with that. In many cases if you made a statement similar to the above on your Facebook page, Twitter or Instagram you would likely receive comments immediately underneath your own post which would quickly be much more extreme and would fall under 'contempt'. This could be problematic for you if you do not remove them from your page.

These rules apply at every stage, from the moment an individual is charged, but they are even more important while a trial is in progress and particularly while the jury is considering a verdict.

While it can be tempting to pass comment, particularly if a tragic incident or terrible crime has occurred in your own community, it is questionable how any statement relating to it can do anything to help your business. The very subject matter is perhaps best avoided on your business social media, but if you feel obliged to reflect what is going on, then perhaps restricting any activity to sharing a link to BBC News website coverage is possibly the safest approach. In particularly challenging times, remember you can temporarily 'Unpublish' your Facebook page or turn off the ability for visitors to comment on posts.

Bullying and harassment

Social media attracts an unpleasant minority who use anonymity to spread hate and misery for others. All the social networks are increasing resources to try and tackle this problem but issues remain.

You may find yourself on the receiving end of unwanted or offensive communication or you may be unfortunate enough to have someone working for you who uses company time and company equipment to engage in such activities.

Again, we would recommend some training to make sure everyone is aware of the risks to themselves and their employment if they are stupid enough to get involved.

Every year, there are dozens of situations where individuals make what they believe are 'jokes' only to find they soon feel the full force of the law as a result. Many others lose their jobs or face disciplinary proceedings for bringing the company into disrepute.

All of this can be avoided, with a simple rule of thumb: if it would be illegal to say it in the street, it's probably illegal to say it on social media. Or before hitting 'publish', ask yourself, 'Would I be happy wearing what I'm about to say on a t-shirt for the rest of my life?', and if the answer is 'No', then think very carefully before publishing it.

Twitter and Instagram may allow anonymous user names but through location tracking and IP address intelligence, not to mention anonymous 'tip offs' from friends and family members, people who thought their identities were hidden can very quickly have them revealed.

The Protection From Harassment (Scotland) Act 1997 states that if an individual makes two unwanted communications towards another individual, they are then guilty of a sustained campaign of harassment. Just two messages constitutes an offence.

Sometimes, of course, the law can be slow to react and we hear of bad situations regularly where people face a torrent of abuse with little apparent action. But it is important to be clear that there are others who quite quickly receive legal punishments.

The best advice we can give is to think very carefully about anything you post and impress upon your staff the need to do the same. Obviously, this applies to any business social media account but equally, anything you say from a personal account can still reflect on your business. Some people will know who you are and where you work; there's also the risk that one day you might get the two accounts muddled up and publish something that might have been OK had it been said by your personal account but most certainly is not OK coming from your business channel.

When your past comes back to haunt you

It's best to treat social media communications as though they are permanent. Of course, Tweets and Facebook updates can be deleted, but if they've been published at all, you do not know how many people have screen captured them or recorded the video with another mobile phone. Once it's out there, there's a strong chance it'll stay out there and that's especially true if the message is controversial, offensive or sexually explicit.

Anything you've said on social media, at any time, can be used against you and the best way to protect yourself is to think very carefully about what you say in the first place. You could also close old accounts (for example, when you move from school into employment, or into a more high profile role) or you could also use one of several apps which allow for 'mass deleting' of previous messages.

I'd advise against relying on these strategies entirely (it's still better not to say the offensive messages in the first place) but at least if you are able to demonstrate that you recognised it as unacceptable and took every reasonable step to remove it as soon as you realised, you will be in a stronger position than if it's still visible on your profile.

!GeekAlert

TweetDelete is a useful tool that enables mass deleting of tweets. While we'd encourage you not to ever need it, we've known it to be used by a wide mix of Twitter account holders including students moving into the world of work, high profile company directors and politicians.

https://bit.ly/etsbook-tweetdelete

Do you have a social media policy?

While it's not a 'get out of jail card' by any measure, if you employ even just one other member of staff, then we strongly recommend having a social media policy. Things they say online could still get the organisation into legal trouble, but if you're able to show the courts (criminal, civil, or employment) that you've tried to provide some best practice social media advice to your staff, then the repercussions on the company should be reduced.

That said, one of the favourite phrases used by a good friend and colleague of ours in the legal profession when it comes to company policies is, 'Live it, don't laminate it'[67]. Don't just hide important information in company policies which stay in a filing cabinet, or are pinned to a company noticeboard. Make sure they're properly communicated, and that staff understand them. Obviously we're biased, but providing social media training to everyone, overlapping with the policy contents, will go a long way to keeping everyone safe and out of trouble.

As for the policy itself, suffice to say we've seen our fair share of them over the years. We've helped create many of them too, and we believe the most effective ones are simple, clear, do not aim to scare the employees, and provide constructive, common sense advice. Treat it more like a social

---

[67] Not that you shouldn't buy a laminator for your company. Every company needs a laminator.

media guidelines document, encouraging both positive social media usage, while raising awareness of the dangers and the ways it can go wrong.

A favourite example that we've used over the years was an older social media policy from the BBC (since updated). Contained within it was guidance not just for the members of staff tasked with doing the actual social media activity, but for all members of staff, regardless of role, based on their own personal social updates. Our favourite part was the simple way it was introduced. It started with the words, 'The following five pages can be summed up with this advice: Don't do anything stupid'. Sometimes staff just need that reminder.

CHAPTER IN A TWEET

Things said on social media can have very serious real-life consequences. One misguided tweet or snapchat post from you or your staff could lead to legal trouble, reputational damage, or financial penalties. Help protect against the risks with a Social Media Policy.

#TrainerLife

Accidental boobs

I think it is testament to our reputation, that so many people we work with, trust us with private information. One such example is passwords. Logins to the likes of Facebook, business websites, email accounts and more, we've been given so many usernames and passwords over the years (often without asking for them!), that had we wanted to, we could have caused some serious havoc.

The truth is, I actually feel a significant degree of pressure being entrusted with such data, in fear of the said login being compromised shortly afterwards, and the client blaming us for it! As such, we always try and remove/delete/rip-up or burn (happened once!) the data quickly after we've completed the work which required it. On this note, keep reading as the next chapter includes advice on better passwords and how to look after them.

As well as passwords, we're regularly entrusted with other private and sensitive data. Business finances, employee grievances, trade secrets and other behind-the-scenes access that wouldn't (and shouldn't) get into the public domain.

Sometimes we see too much.

Sometimes we're given access to personal mobile phones under the premise of 'please show me how to upload a photo to Instagram' and in doing so we stumble across images that other people really shouldn't ever see.

Accidental viewings of boobs, bums and bits have lately been commonplace, so much so that I'm wondering if it's now mandatory to take them if you own a mobile phone.

Having a trainer see such private photos is one thing, having everyone in the training room see them is another – so please people, if you DO have such visuals on your device, don't agree to the trainer connecting your phone to the projector so that 'everyone can benefit from me showing them your issue'. It's not your issue that I'm showing them, and there are no benefits!

Gary

14

Cyber security

(and the steps to protect against anti-social behaviour)

Gary

The very nature of social media means you are 'putting yourself out there' and when you do that, there's always a risk.

Businesses create social media profiles because they want attention. They then start using them to interact and increasingly to do business. So, hairdressing salons, restaurants and vehicle repair centres all take bookings and discuss transactions via Twitter Direct Messages or Facebook Messenger conversations. And there are many business interactions via LinkedIn.

So there's a lot at stake if that information falls into someone else's hands, or if you were to find yourself suddenly locked out of your own account.

> **66** There are only two types of companies: those that have been hacked, and those that will be. **99**
> **Robert Mueller, former FBI Director**

Latest figures show that almost half of all UK businesses suffered some sort of cyber attack last year.

The bigger the business, the more likely they are to suffer an attack but it is clear that even small, micro, sole trader and new start businesses also suffer attacks and the consequences can be disastrous. Even if there's no significant immediate financial loss, the time taken to recover and the reputational damage as you inform customers as to what has happened, can be impossible to recover from.

What does a cyber attack even look like?

Cyber attacks take many forms. A hacker gaining access to your website could take it offline, costing you a vital marketing channel but for ecommerce businesses this would actually prevent you from doing business at all for a period of time. In more serious cases, recovering your website might mean the loss of data or customer details being compromised, which is very serious and you then have very important responsibilities under the GDPR legislation[68].

There are phishing scams where rogue emails look like they come from an official source but are in fact scams, designed to get you to click and download files which then infect your computer with malware. This can lead to keystrokes being recorded, giving hackers access to passwords, and sometimes even banking information, and in other cases pop-up ads which quickly cripple your computer and leave you unable to do anything online.

Phishing doesn't just happen via email, with social media impersonation massively on the rise right now. Are you 100% sure that the Twitter reply from your bank is indeed them? Of course it must be – you initiated the conversation and they've replied promptly – excellent customer service!

Check, and then check again![69]

---

[68] We promise not to go into any detail on GDPR, but suffice to say it's hugely important you understand the basics and how it impacts your business: https://bit.ly/etsbook-gdpr
[69] The real risk of Twitter ranting: https://bit.ly/etsbook-twitterrant

*Case Study - Virgrim Media

Proving how easy it is to be taken in by an elaborate social scam, Colin's kindly agreed to tell his own story of how he very nearly got into a lot of trouble. In his own words:

My wife was out at her yoga class one evening and I was making dinner for myself and our two children. Multi-tasking is not my thing, so I'd put the boys in front of the television to keep them occupied, which meant I could get on with the tricky business of keeping an eye on the waffles in the oven, sausages on the grill and frozen vegetables on the hob. Like I said, multi-tasking isn't my thing and this was me working at maximum capacity.

Our youngest came running in, in the midst of all this to inform me that the Virgin Media box wasn't working and the on demand episode of 'PJ Masks', or whatever it was they were watching, wasn't working. Being the highly motivated action orientated kind of guy that I am, I took immediate action and tweeted Virgin Media, asking if I could Direct Message (DM) them to tell them about this fault. 30 seconds later, I received a private message from Virgrim Media, to say I could go ahead and they were now following me.

I explained the fault, (having turned the waffles over) then gave the veg a quick stir before following up with my name and address. The friendly employee on the other side sent a DM back explaining they were just accessing my account details and could I confirm my identity by typing the 16 digits from the front of my debit card, the expiry date and three digits on the back.

I started typing the information they'd asked for and somewhere between the expiry date and the three digits on the back something struck me. Why did Virgin Media need that information? I pay by direct debit. The card wouldn't have any information that would be of any use to them. Unless....

I came out of the direct message and clicked on the sender's profile picture. It looked like Virgin Media, it had all their branding over it, but hang on...they'd only sent six tweets. The account did not have a blue tick. And when I looked really closely, I saw the Twitter user name and realised, to my horror, I hadn't been speaking to Virgin Media at all, but rather to Virgrim Media which was using a very smart 'cloned' page to hoodwink people into giving up their personal information.

'You cheeky bast***!' I typed. 'Be careful with the language', came the reply, 'Remember I know where you live.'

As I served the kids their tea I realised what a lucky escape I'd had and how stupid I had been. Not treating social media with respect – thinking I could bash out a quick complaint on social media and quickly resolve a technical problem while being responsible for my children and cooking a meal. That's asking for trouble. You might be able to handle doing three things at once but I can't. Perhaps getting a bit complacent about cyber-security: thinking I knew all the scams and no-one would ever catch me out. But I was also pleased that the conversations I've had (many with Gary) and all that I've read had actually sunk in and I'd managed to stop myself from sharing those sensitive details which could have cost me dear.

I told Gary what had happened a few days later and he explained he'd heard of many cases like this, where someone tweets a well-known brand with a 'customer service' related issue. The operator of the rogue, cloned account sees the public tweet first and initiates a reply, via DM. All the victim sees is the logo and username (which they recognise) in their messages folder and so the conversation begins. There's even a setting in Twitter which can prevent this – just select 'Only People I Follow Can Send Me Direct Messages'.

When it comes to cyber security, learning from other people's mistakes is a great strategy, so I hope you will learn from mine. It always happens when you least expect it and this type of crime is very much on the rise, especially with so many of us now hyper aware around emails and text messages. Direct Messages on social media platforms are the next big area of risk.

If you think it can't happen to you, you are almost certainly wrong. But there's a lot you can do to protect yourself. First is making sure any devices, systems, software or programmes you are using are always updated to the most recent version. That way you can be sure you are covered by the most up to date security protection and any known flaws have been patched.

One of the simplest things you can do to protect yourself is to use a better, more secure password. More of that further on. We would also recommend the use of '2 factor authentication' (or 2FA) wherever it is available. Put it on your websites, social media profiles and email. This is a relatively unobtrusive (and free) system where the provider recognises a log in attempt from a location you don't normally use. In this case, as well as inputting your user name and password, you also require a six digit pin code sent to you mobile phone before you are allowed access. If it is you, accessing your own email or website then you'll almost certainly have access to your mobile phone, and so inputting the code won't be a problem. The vast majority of cyber attacks are remote. The perpetrator doesn't have access to your mobile and so even though they may have a super computer at their disposal which has cracked your password, they are still unable to access your properties. Most two step verification systems will also notify you of any log in attempt so you'll know when you're under attack and can quickly take the required action.

With cyber crime only increasing, take steps now to prepare. Make sure you regularly back up your files, think not just about security but resilience — how quickly could you recover if your systems were destroyed? What data and work would be lost and how would you get it back? Beware the threat within too — what access do your staff have? Restrict this where necessary and make sure you know who has access to what and where.

The need for better passwords

I'm guessing that as a responsible business person, you're not in the habit of just leaving the office keys lying around for anyone to pocket. I'm guessing that if you're in retail, you don't leave the safe door open at night, allowing anyone walking past the window to see the day's takings inside[70]. And I'd even take a bet that your bicycle combination lock isn't still set to "0-0-0-0" which was the default when you purchased it.

Why then do so many people have a really terrible attitude to passwords. Trust me – most of us take more care and concern over our mountain bikes getting stolen than we do our data. And unless you have a seriously impressive mountain bike[71], your data is worth significantly more, and not just in monetary terms.

Many of the 'dangers' highlighted earlier are mitigated with a robust company password policy. Implementing a better password is often the simplest thing you can do to massively increase your chances of staying safe (or put it another way, to massively decrease your chances of becoming a victim). And if you're reading this thinking to yourself, 'but who'd want to hack me....I've got nothing really of value.... feel free to log in to my email and tidy up my inbox for me....etc.' (and I've heard all this before from people who seriously weren't joking) then you need this advice more than most, as you're the biggest threat to the company right now.

The truth is, this might possibly be the most important section in the whole book, since all the 'good stuff' that's gone before is instantly undone if you're hacked, and you'd be surprised how often that happens to small businesses every single day.

So rather than just shout at you, I'll pass on my three top tips to a better password.

1. Use a better password.

Really? That's the top tip? YES it is. Just start using a better password. Intuitively you know your password is rubbish. You know you gave it little thought. And if you don't realise this, then here's a few disturbing facts for you.

---

[70] Can I suggest that if you have a safe, you actually don't position it near the window at all, open door or not.
[71] I used to have a brilliant designer called Paul work for me, and I was continually amazed at how much money he spent on bikes #JustSaying.

If your password is based on a word in the dictionary, a hacker is likely to crack you 'instantly'. They'll run what's called a dictionary attack on your account, trying every word in the English language[72] from 1000's of different slave computers, gaining access in no time.

But it's ok, because you don't do that do you. And if you do, at least you capitalise the first letter, and add the number 1 at the end. You don't just use the word holidays as your password, you beef it up to *Holidays1* or perhaps you use a two digit number at the end – your year of birth, or the current year? Well done. Your *Holidays86* password just gained you a few hours of protection.

You might take it further, replacing every letter 'o' with a zero, and replacing every 's' with a $. You're really proud of your *H0liday$86* password aren't you? Until I tell you that all these obvious substitutions are even more obvious to the hackers, and you've now increased your protection to maybe a few days, but it's certainly anything but 'strong' (despite the fact your system highlighted it as 'strong' and the wee bar went 'green').

At this stage, can I just point out that rarely does a hacker sit at his/ her[73] desk typing in different words manually. Rarely are you a specific target (although more on that later). What's more likely is that you are unfortunately on the hacker's list today (along with millions of others) and his/her supercomputer[74] is running 1000s of combinations every second, hoping that a few idiots on the list do what every other idiot does, which is the same thing.

Patterns are easy to guess by computers. Complete randomness is not. So here are two methods I'd suggest to help you come up with a unique random password that (while not impossible to crack – nothing is!) will make it a damn sight more difficult to predict, and hopefully have the computer 'timing out' and moving onto the next target on the list.

---

[72] Other languages too, even Klingon.

[73] If the images on Pixabay.com are anything to go by, all hackers are male, and nearly always wear a dark hoodie.

[74] Which I can confirm does definitely not resemble the friendly looking Supercomputer from Ant and Dec's Saturday Night Takeaway.

Strong password technique one:

Take a look around you, and identify three random things that don't go together. For example: Alexa, Poinsettia[75], and Coffee. Stick them together and say hello to your new password: AlexaPoinsettiaCoffee. According to www.howsecureismypassword.net[76] this will take 861 quadrillion years to crack, and I think that's quite a long time. Make it even better with the same number substitutions as discussed earlier. Almost bullet-proof!

Strong password technique two:

If I told you that one of my passwords was M2grcJ&J1lt2b![77] then you're probably thinking 'Wow Gary, that's a really secure random password'. You're half right; it is secure (crackable in 204 million years supposedly), but it's not random, not to me anyway. To everyone else (including the computer hacking scripts) it looks like a completely random series of 14 characters; to me it means something. It's based on a phrase: 'My 2 girls are called Janice and Janine I love them to bits!'. You get the point......

And finally, before we move on to the other tips, please don't forget about the password to access your mobile phone. Most people don't have one. At best they have a four digit code, or a 'pattern they swipe' with their finger on the screen (and which when anyone picks up the phone to examine, the pattern is immediately obvious!).

Take a minute and think about the implications of someone gaining access to your smart phone. How many apps do you have on there that are business related? How many apps give 'instant access' without any further login requirements? Think about Facebook; once you're past the phone's log in screen, it doesn't then ask you to log into Facebook, it's simply straight in, with access to post on your profile, your business page, and to engage with all your customers. It's the same for most apps; easy access to everything, once I bypass your phone's four digit passcode. At the very least, change the four digits to six digits. Better than that, change it to an actual strong 'alpha-numeric' password reinforced with

---

[75] Yes, I'm writing this chapter at Christmas; I don't normally have Poinsettias just lying around.
[76] Have a play with it, just don't give it your actual password to check!
[77] Stop trying to hack me on Facebook – that's not my password.

fingerprint or facial recognition (all done within the phone's security settings). Just don't make it the same password you use elsewhere. Which leads me to my second tip (some might call it a rant)...

2. Stop using the same password for different things.

Hands up if you'll admit to using the same password for more than one login?[78] You are not alone. Most people do this, and when I tell them to immediately stop such a dangerous practice, they scowl and curse me!

We all do it because it's convenient. After all, who can remember the dozens of logins[79] we all have on the internet, and if each one had a different password we'd spend more time trying (and failing) to log in to things than actually using them. The solution – just use the same password for different things.

So here's the thing. Even if you follow my advice in tip one, and generate an amazing super-secure password, because you're using it in multiple places, it's immediately insecure.

Because while YOU look after the password, and ensure it never falls into the wrong hands, others won't. Popular airlines, hotel chains, telecoms companies, social networks, cloud storage platforms, retailers and more[80], have all had high-profile hacks in recent months and years where customer data was stolen – potentially your data. In some cases, this included passwords. Yes, your amazing 'AlexaPoinsettiaCoffee' password is out in the open, not just in the hands of the hacker who stole it, but now on the dark web, available for purchase by other criminal gangs and baddies (all wearing hoodies).

What do they do with the data? With one click, your username and password is literally tried on every other log in page on the internet. And because you like the convenience of having just one password, they've

---

[78] Colin just reminded me that this is a book, not a workshop full of people, and that 'hands up' requests are pretty pointless. Regardless, if you did put your hand up (or even considered doing it) thank you for playing along.
[79] Some studies suggest that we all have over 100 online accounts, each requiring a username and password.
[80] Not for the paranoid! Take a look at the names listed here, and you'll realise your data has already been exploited: https://bit.ly/etsbook-hacks

got you. Everywhere. It's a thought that doesn't bear thinking about, but you need to think about it because the damage can be disastrous. Why? Because now it's targeted. Now the hackers are coming after you with intent.

On a personal level you now have criminals accessing your Amazon account, buying things on your credit card, on your Facebook trying to convince your friends to 'click here' on Messenger, and on your GMail deleting your life's history in emails, while spamming everyone in your address book at the same time, telling them you're stuck in the Congo and need some money transferred to your bank account straight away.

From a business perspective it gets worse. All your files stolen from your DropBox, including your own customer data (there's a GDPR fine coming soon, not to mention all the negative PR and angry customers you're about to get), your suppliers all emailed (from you) asking them to change bank details, your website access details changed and (just for good measure) the homepage defaced, and your Twitter account compromised, and, as in the case of one major fast food burger chain a few years ago – your customers told where the beef really comes from!

It's not funny, especially if it happens to you. And it will (to some extent) if you keep using the same password on different sites. Stop it now please.

If you're really struggling with this idea, and you're stressing out how you're going to manage over 100 random passwords, then fear not. I'll give you a solution for this shortly, but here's another wee 'hack' that might help: although the cyber security purists out there might have a hissy fit at me for sharing this, as it's not considered best practice (but will still probably be significantly more secure that what you're currently doing!).

If your new strong password is 'AlexaPoinsettiaCoffee', then don't come up with 100 different passwords like this, come up with a system. So if you're logging into Facebook, maybe your password simply becomes 'FalexaPoinsettiaCoffeeB' (the password wrapped in FB). If logging into LinkedIn, then it's 'LalexaPoinsettiaCoffeel'. You hopefully get the point.

As I mentioned, it's not best practice, and if a hacker is really out to get you and is manually trying things, they might crack your system, but in the knowledge that 99% of these types of hacks happen automatically[81], with people getting into trouble because they are using the SAME password on different sites, well now you're safer than all those careless 'I can't remember 100 passwords' people, and have hugely increased your chances of staying safe online.

3. Use a Password Manager.

If I try and give a proper technical explanation as to why using a Password Manager is a very good idea to help protect your online systems, then I guarantee the next few paragraphs would be very geeky indeed. Suffice to say that if you do use one, you're significantly better protected than most.

In simple terms, a Password Manager is a bit of software (either installed on your device, or accessed via the cloud) which holds ALL of your passwords. To access them, you just need to remember the 'master password' used by the software. At this point you might be thinking this sounds bonkers! ALL of your passwords, stored in one system! That's worse than having a Big Red Book of passwords[82] sitting on the office shelf! What if that system gets hacked?

Well, if the system does get hacked, the data the bad guys get is nonsense because it's all encrypted. And the only way to unencrypt[83] it is with your master password, which isn't stored anywhere other than inside your head (so don't forget it!). That's a quick (and not very good) explanation of Password Managers. There's loads of them, and you should do your own research to decide which brand to use (some free, some paid), but to get you started, take a look at Dashlane, LastPass, KeePass and My1Login.

There's lots more you can do with regards to better passwords. We've already mentioned 2FA[84] and the benefits of having a dedicated Password policy across your organisation (a requirement if you're hoping

---

[81] I just made that statistic up. If anyone wants to supply a more accurate number for the second edition of this book, feel free.
[82] Yes, I once visited a client who had one of these. And it was indeed Red.
[83] Or 'decrypt' as the cyber experts would say.
[84] What do you mean you've forgotten what this acronym stands for already? Two Factor Authentication.

to achieve 'Cyber Essentials' certification[85]), but I think it best to end this section here because I suspect I'm beginning to risk losing you. That said, if you've picked up this book, and are reading this just before bed time, you're welcome.

Zoom Bombing

And finally (with a last minute addition to this chapter) we couldn't not mention the fairly recent phenomenon that is Zoom Bombing! A phrase that prior to COVID-19 lockdown you'd probably never heard of, but now might be among your biggest concerns if you're running public webinars (and if you're not, read Chapter 7 which explains why you maybe should!).

The truth is, Zoom Bombing[86] isn't actually (despite what the media sometimes claim) anything to do with hacking, insecure systems, or even passwords. It's to do with people, and a lack of care when hosting online events. At best, 'Zoom Bombing' involves people you wouldn't expect to join, gaining access to an online meeting and behaving inappropriately during it. It could be as simple as students joining a remote lesson anonymously, who go on to make a fool of the teacher, spamming the live chat facility or drawing rude shapes with a virtual pen on the shared screen. At worst, it involves organised groups of sex offenders forcing the absolute worst material imaginable onto the participants on your session.

How does it happen? A mix of naivety on the part of some session organisers and malicious intent on behalf of the perpetrators. The truth is, what we're talking about could happen on any online video sharing platform, it's just that the majority of it, the worst offences, most of the damage, happens to occur on Zoom.

A few simple steps can greatly reduce the chances of this happening to you. And it's all about balancing your need to control what goes on in your session, with a desire to make it easy for participants to access.

---

[85] Cyber Essentials is worth looking at, especially if you work with public sector clients.
[86] Which we've seen happen to organisations of all shapes and sizes, both in the public and private sectors.

Many 'Zoom Bombing' incidents occur because an online meeting organiser shares a link to the session on social media. Depending on how the session is configured, that might mean absolutely anyone with the link can click it and immediately join the session. Once they're in, if you've given everyone the ability to share their camera and screen, then they can share whatever malicious content they want to everyone else. It's easy to avoid this. The first action is to carefully control who gets into your sessions. Most platforms offer a 'waiting room' facility, where participants are forced to verify their identity, you can then check off their names and admit them one at a time to the session. You can then 'lock' the meeting and prevent anyone else gaining access. You can also password protect sessions (after recent security concerns many webinar and video conferencing platforms now require a password by default). This eliminates the risk of automated bots, scraping the internet, looking for public Zoom meeting links, joining and automatically streaming pornography into the session. That's right – some of the worst perpetrators of Zoom Bombing are machines rather than people.

You can keep sessions public but minimise the risk simply by restricting participants' ability to share webcams, join before the host and automatically share their screen. There's an inherent danger in making online interactive sessions TOO accessible. Before you do anything, you should get familiar with the various settings and options and take advice if you're unsure. Getting it wrong can have a negative impact on your brand and might leave you open to some serious complaints and safeguarding issues.

These issues have received so much negative coverage there's no excuse now for being caught out. Err on the side of caution and show the same level of concern for the well-being of your online virtual participants as you would for anyone you work with face to face in the physical world. It strikes me that Health and Safety considerations should extend to online and just as any 'event' in the physical world would be subject to a risk assessment, so, perhaps should any online event. As I hope we've explained, so many of the risks and dangers can be greatly reduced with good planning and a few simple actions.

CHAPTER IN A TWEET

Protect your business from the risks of cyber attack by educating yourself, and your staff. Ensure best practice password management, understand how to improve security settings in systems you use, and always be aware that you are a target for some anti-social behaviour.

15

Learning from the data

(and why you should never measure hits)

Gary and Colin

Everything digital can be measured. It's ones and zeros. It's there or it's not. Anything that happens online, on your social media platforms or on your website can be tracked and measured, recorded and compared.

In the early days of the internet, many websites had 'hit counters' on the bottom which simply showed how many times the page had been visited since the counter was installed. But what use is this? What would 10,000,000 hits on your website mean[87]? Would it sell anything? Would it make you money? Or grow the business?

The number on its own doesn't mean anything. But if you know that people who read a particular blog post you had written, were more likely to then watch your promotional video and download a free PDF you had created, and that of those who downloaded and read the PDF, a significant majority went on to sign-up and become lucrative customers, spending large amounts of money with you, then you would be interested in that, wouldn't you? The data would mean something. Because you would know that your promotional video was good, that your PDF was serving a purpose and that a particular type of blog post was successful in attracting, not just an audience that visited your webpage, but the right audience, full of people who become customers and actually spend money with you.

That's where we want to get to and that's what modern data or analytics is all about.

What data are you collecting?

The first step is making sure you have the ability to gather the data in the first place. That means installing Google Analytics on your website. It's a free, simple piece of code that takes less than a minute to set up and then copy and paste into your site. Other more sophisticated analytics tools are available but we think everyone should start with this. Create an account and sign up at http://analytics.google.com and follow the step-by-step instructions.

---

[87] HITS = How Idiots Track Success. Don't take that too personally if that's what you've been using to measure your website success, but make sure you speak to us immediately so we can explain the error of your ways!

When the code is installed on your site, you should also display a 'This website uses cookies' warning when your site loads. There are plug-ins and templates you can choose which enable this; have a word with your web designer to get this set up and ensure you comply with the GDPR regulations[88]. All the main social media platforms will gather data for you when your account goes live. What it all means for you depends on your business objectives and what you actually want social media to do for you.

If it is simply brand awareness and making sure people know you exist, then something as simple as the 'reach' on each post would be of interest. The higher that number, the better things are. But you would probably quickly want more sophisticated insight. It's not just 'anyone' seeing the material, it's a particular type of person, in a particular location, with a particular set of interests, that's probably what you really want. And how does that number change over time?

This is especially important in larger businesses with marketing teams or where this activity is outsourced to someone else. Is it working? Is this week better than last week? Are the posts Colin published getting a better result than those that Gary creates? Tracking and measuring this over time allows you to make intelligence-based business decisions. You would know which of your social media channels delivers the more lucrative audience. Not simply the one with the highest numbers but the one doing the most to deliver against your business objectives.

The data provided also shows you where your followers are, what time of the day or night they are active, and which of your posts they engaged with the most. In short, you learn what works and what doesn't and with a commitment to continual improvement, you can do more of what works and less of what doesn't. That way your business is always making progress.

Data to check out

One of my favourite bits of data is 'Who's viewed your Profile' on LinkedIn.

---

[88] Gary just pointed out to me that I've committed an 'ATM Machine' faux pas. Confused? Me too!

Users of LinkedIn's free tier are restricted to viewing data on the five most recent users who have looked at your profile. If you pay, you have access to them all. This is often a useful early warning of who is about to approach your business and make an enquiry, or at least people most likely to be willing to accept a connection request from you. You can also use this the other way. For example, if there is another business person I identify and I would like for them to know I exist, then assuming they are also interested in who is looking at their page, I only need to click their name and look at their profile, and BOOM!, they now know I have looked and when they read the 'headline text' underneath my name, they will know what I do. And, while it doesn't happen this way every time, on many occasions they will then ask to connect with me, which of course is exactly what I wanted to happen in the first place.

Data from email newsletters can be useful too. What time of the day leads to the highest open rate? Do funny subject lines get a better response than straightforward ones? What links get the most clicks? All this information can be extremely useful for businesses, but data can be overwhelming and it's not something you should get too hung up on.

Businesses that come to our Embrace The Space workshop tend to be smaller businesses and many don't have a dedicated marketing department. So our advice, once the systems are installed and set up, is to pay attention to no more than two or three key metrics at any one time and concentrate on them. For example, if you are an online retailer you might want to increase the number of pages (products) the average visitor looks at per session. So adding a 'related products' section at the foot of each page would make sense and might help with this. If you wanted to educate your customers you might write some blog posts explaining the benefits of your products and services and so you would expect to see the 'duration' of the average session increase. And if you had a sophisticated sales funnel set up you'd expect to see visitors coming to the site and consuming content, then performing a conversion (clicking on a button, visiting a contact form etc.) and ultimately going deeper into your business and eventually becoming a customer.

On social media, we've seen some businesses get tremendous results simply by changing the time of day they post. Their Facebook insights show them when their audience is most online and by experimenting with times, e.g. 0730, 1130 and 2130, you can see which time of day gets the highest reach and then move things around to get better results. While Facebook allows direct scheduling of posts from its 'Creator Studio', for Twitter, LinkedIn and other networks, this can be done from a social media management tool such as Hootsuite or Buffer.

The key thing is to understand is what data can be measured and collected, and then to connect the elements which are of interest to you, to business objectives such as leads, enquiries and the most important one of all, money in your account.

Stop making assumptions about how your channels are working, and dig deeper into all the available data.

!GeekAlert

While some platforms like Facebook and Instagram have some great insights built-in to show you audience activity based on time of day (allowing you to post at times to better suit them), others like Twitter lack these facilities. Enter FollowerWonk[89] – a brilliant third party website which gives you a huge amount of valuable Twitter data, which Twitter itself fails to do.

Head over to https://followerwonk.com/ and create yourself a free account, then start analysing your own Twitter followers, or the followers of any other Twitter account (handy for knowing when your competitor's customers are most active!). Twitter is still essentially a chronological 'real-time' platform (if people don't see it when you post it, they'll likely never see it), so posting at the right time is arguably more important here than on other (more algorithmic driven) platforms. FollowerWonk gives you this data, and much more – all for free. You should try it!

---

[89] Don't shoot the messenger – I realise it's a stupid name!

CHAPTER IN A TWEET

Without data, there is just assumption. Don't assume you know what happens on your website or social media. Prove it! Work out what you want to know, and how to measure it. For some, data might not be a sexy topic[90], but understanding it is vital to your business success.

---

[90] For those of you who do find data sexy, I can recommend some professional support.

16

Social media in the mainstream media

(and how to grab headlines in the real world)

Colin

When it's done well, social media can achieve impressive audience numbers. Some businesses we've worked with have received tens of thousands, and sometimes even hundreds of thousands of views for something they've shared.

But for many businesses the numbers are much smaller. And 'reach' on social media alone won't bring success to your business. Chances are you need something more specific such as new relationships, sales enquiries or money in your account.

What if there was something else that could build on your use of social media but take it to new heights, with bigger audiences, and put you in front of influential people who could hold the key to transforming your business? That something is the mainstream media.

Get your business in a newspaper or on television or radio and you'll be perceived differently. People will assume you must be doing well. People will tell you they saw it and congratulate you. People you haven't heard from in ages, or who you don't know at all, will suddenly want to talk to you.

I'm assuming this hypothetical coverage is for something positive, rather than something like a health and safety breach (there is such a thing as bad publicity and you should avoid it), and keep in mind one 'media mention' on its own is unlikely to bring benefits right away. But it all builds up. Journalists can be a bit like sheep; if a reporter writes a story about you in a newspaper, that might lead to radio coverage, which might even lead to a TV news item – it goes round and round because a herd mentality can grow up around a single story.

And while newspaper circulation is not like it used to be, certain titles are still read by influential people who it can be useful to have on your side. Sometimes, simply having the right people knowing you exist can bring opportunities your way.

Experience has taught me that if you innovate in the digital space, you can receive mainstream media coverage. Do something clever, funny, interesting, dangerous, novel or exciting on the internet and there's a very high chance a newspaper, radio or television channel will become interested enough to cover it. Get coverage in one outlet and others are likely to follow, giving you free exposure to an audience likely to make your competitors green with envy.

Journalists on Twitter

Journalists use social media as a source of stories. And many use Twitter. Pick a newspaper you would like to be featured in and search for Twitter profiles of journalists who work there. Over the next few weeks occasionally 'like', 'reply', or 'retweet' something they say. Slowly but surely you are getting on their radar. Tag them in on posts you publish, if you think they would be interested. Make sure your biography does you justice and says something that might grab a journalist's interest. So rather than, 'We have 40 years' experience manufacturing packaging materials', you might say 'Scotland's happiest packaging manufacturer – for a cleaner, greener world'. Now, a journalist looking for case studies of businesses committed to improving the environment might be interested in learning more about you.

Ideally, you want these journalists to follow you back. When they do that, you can of course direct message them, start a dialogue and begin to build a relationship which in time, could lead to free, positive publicity about your business. But here's the reality check: 'We've won an award', 'We're relaunching our website' and 'Sale now on' are unlikely to be of interest to a decent journalist.

I was going to write a sentence here about how I believe journalists are inherently lazy but our editor/proofreader (we're paying her for one but pleaded with her to do both) is proving to be trickier to get round than I thought, so let me pre-empt her red pen and say that when I was a journalist, I was lazy.

And Twitter would have been an absolute godsend. Think about it. No need to trawl the contacts book and phone people up trying to 'find' stories. No need to leave my desk. I would simply bring up Twitter, find some businesses that follow me and direct message them. 'Hey, are you up to anything interesting? Do you have any stories? I see you recently shared a post on Twitter about your 1,000th customer, can you tell me some more about that?'. There's a large amount of what you read in newspapers that comes from exactly that sort of dialogue.

So social media is an effective way of getting to know journalists but I also believe many journalists have a fascination with all things digital. It's a subject matter that audiences enjoy reading about and hearing about.

As I said, innovate in the digital space and you will often receive mainstream media coverage.

Here are three quick examples of businesses which did something interesting or clever online and received newspaper coverage as a result.

1. McDonald's Snapchat recruitment.

The fast food giant announced it would be taking job applications via Snapchat, where applicants had to 'snap' a picture of themselves using a specially created filter which put them in the McDonald's uniform complete with name badge. This lead to typical 'outrage' from sections of the media expressing their disgust that something as serious and formal as recruiting for a post was now going to be decided by something as flippant as 'who's got the best selfie?'. The truth was somewhat more subtle in that the Snapchat pictures were merely the first stage in the recruitment process (you sent your selfie then received the application pack which continued along traditional lines) but the resulting media coverage gave McDonald's huge levels of free recruitment advertising and ensured that a huge chunk of the working population (not just Snapchat users) knew they were looking for staff.

2. UNICEF and Pinterest.

This campaign won a lot of support and involved the charity UNICEF working with Ami Musa to create a board on Pinterest titled 'Really Want These'.

Ami was 13 at the time, and lived in Sierra Leone, one of the countries where UNICEF was concentrating its campaigning. The objective was to encourage people to donate and support the work the charity was doing there.

Most Pinterest users have aspirational Pinterest boards where they highlight places they'd like to go, clothes and products they would hope to buy one day. So you might expect to see a beautiful holiday destination, a trendy pair of jeans, some make-up, a fast, flashy car etc. But for Ami, and many others like her in Sierra Leone, her 'Wants' were different. Her Pinterest board featured a bar of soap, a chalkboard in a classroom (representing education), some clean water running into a bucket, and some food to eat.

The juxtaposition of this glitzy, glamourous channel being used by someone who would so appreciate life's bare essentials had a huge impact. And while it did gain some traction on social media, where it really got attention was when the Daily Mail discovered it and ran an article on what UNICEF had done. That's where the real benefits came.

3. The Global Rich List.

Our final example, and another charity. This time it's CARE. Every year, after the Sunday Times Rich List is published, CARE asks social media users, 'Where are you on the Global Rich List?'. Click on the social media posts and you land on a special website where users are asked to enter their annual salary.

They then see a slick animation which shows, in relative terms, how much better off they are, compared to everyone else on the planet. Anyone earning the average UK salary would be comfortably within the top 1.5% highest earners out of seven billion people in the world.

The interactive graphics explain the income inequality which impacts our world, and of course, explains the work CARE is doing to address this and how you can help. It's a powerful, interactive and very personal method of getting the message across and again, always generates attention in the mainstream media.

Giving people something to do is always worth aiming for and can get some amazing results.

While the above three examples are from bigger, well known brands, getting into the media through innovative use of digital marketing is something many small businesses can achieve. Gary managed it with his social media stunt 'The Paypal Visit' which showed how a creative idea carried out on Facebook could attract the press and achieve wider public attention.

Make the internal, external

I'm aware this sounds like something terrible a surgeon[91] might say in a horror film, but I want you to remember it. I think too many businesses create an unnecessary division between 'internal' and 'external' comms. Some even have different departments to handle these comms, and go to great lengths to have a particular dialogue with their own staff, and an entirely different discussion with customers and the public.

In this age of transparency, I think it's better to be as open as possible. In fact, much of what some businesses might think should be kept 'internal' could work really well if it was made public and shared through social media channels.

Premier Inn owner Whitbread, supermarket giant ASDA, and local authorities such as Renfrewshire Council and Hull City Council, are examples of organisations using public social media to talk to their staff.

For several years now, Scottish Swimming has produced its annual report[92] as a YouTube video. It contains all the facts and figures you'd expect from such a document but the pictures, music and scrolling text really bring the report to life and generate a lot of goodwill for the organisation.

CHAPTER IN A TWEET

Traditional media is full of stories about how businesses are using digital platforms and many journalists are active on Twitter. Seemingly mundane business material can earn a new lease of life if it is repurposed for social media and shared publicly.

---

[91] Like Hacksaw Harry from Chapter 10.
[92] View it here: https://bit.ly/etsbook-scottishswimming

#TrainerLife

Woeful wifi

A few years ago, we'd been booked to deliver our full day Embrace The Space workshop, and, as always when the client asks us about our room requirements, broadband internet access was near the top of our list.

We turned up on the morning of the event and got to work setting things up. It was certainly a top class hotel, in a beautiful location and the staff seemed friendly and helpful.

The room was equipped with the requisite big screen to plug into, there was plenty of space and having caught a glimpse of the lunch menu on our way in, I was looking forward to a great day.

And so it came as something of a surprise when Gary scanned his available wireless networks and no hotel wifi came up.

'Don't worry', Gary said. 'It's probably hidden, it'll be a secure, hidden network, they'll set us up if we ask for it'.

I could see where he was coming from, as we'd experienced this in a few places previously. Like Government HQ. It did seem a bit strange for a city centre hotel.

Help arrived moments later in the shape of a member of hotel staff. He came breezing in and asked us if everything was OK.

'Yeah, it's great', I said, 'But could you give us the wifi network when you get a chance.'

Our man's face fell.

'There isn't really wifi in this room', he said.'

By 'isn't really', what he meant was, 'there isn't any'.

Now, this would have been bad enough, given it was something our client had specifically asked for.

But it was his ingenious proposed solution that had us in stitches.

Clearly, having experienced top notch customer service training, and seeing that this was such an important issue to us, our man went the extra mile and proposed a solution neither of us were expecting.

We watched open mouthed as he strode over to the window and pulled back the huge, heavy curtain with a flourish.

'Look at that!', he said, beaming.

We looked down to see some passengers boarding the Number 16 bus. 'The buses all have free wifi', he said with a nod. 'And you can pick it up from here. It's an open network, no password and there's almost always a bus sitting there. You should get on no bother.'

Thankfully, our city centre location meant both our phones received first class 3G coverage (I told you we'd been doing this for a while), so we thanked the bloke for his help and tethered up.

Colin

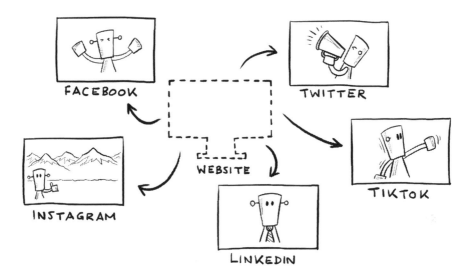

17

Why your website still matters

(and the importance of blogging)

Colin

As he sometimes reminds me when he's feeling nostalgic, Gary has designed and built a fair few websites in his life. He knows his HTML from his CSS. His Javascript from his GeoCities. And don't get him started on 'Million Dollar Homepage' which he even bought some pixels on.

Anyway, with so many people using social media platforms and the ever expanding feature set they offer, there's a perfectly legitimate question we get asked a lot: 'If we're using social media, does my business still need a website?'.

Our answer, and I don't see it changing anytime soon, is always, 'Yes'.

We fully appreciate many businesses across a wide variety of sectors get all their leads and customer engagement through platforms like Instagram, LinkedIn and Facebook. Many new-start, sole trader businesses, including many that start as hobbies and then become more full-time ventures, can build very strong customer bases on social media.

You certainly don't NEED a website to succeed in business these days, and having one certainly doesn't mean success is any more likely.

But given the opportunity, in an ideal world, you should have a website to complement what you're doing on your chosen social networks.

Why you still need a website

The thinking behind this is simple. Your website is something you own. No matter how successful your Facebook or Instagram account might be, it isn't yours. It could disappear at any time. It seems unlikely just now of course but Facebook could go bust, it could get hacked, kick you off for saying something that breaks its terms and conditions, or simply make it harder for you to get the reach you want.

We live in a fast moving and ever changing world. Think of how much things have changed in the last ten years. It would be foolish to try to predict the next few years.

And so we think a website provides your business with an anchor in these turbulent times. It doesn't need to do much, and certainly doesn't need to cost you a lot of money, but having it could prove to be a valuable asset.

You'll have heard about fake news and the issue of trust online. It's incredibly easy for people to create fake social media accounts in your business name. Have you taken your TikTok user name yet? Or Snapchat? If you haven't, I could take it right now and pass myself off as you. How would your customers know the difference?

If you had an official, established website, you would have some form of protection.

That website would contain links to your official profiles on social media. It gives the audience a place to verify who you actually are. And makes it much easier for them to find you on the various platforms you use.

If you believe many potential customers find your business via a Google search, then your website can help in a way Facebook, Twitter and Instagram might not be able to. As we explain in the Search Engine Optimisation bonus chapter later, Google does not fully index Instagram, for example. So if your objective is to climb the Google rankings, Instagram is unlikely to be able to help. Whereas a website with well written pages, and perhaps the addition of a blog section, would make a serious impact and take you higher up Google rankings.

There might be certain functions on your website that you don't want to handover to a social networking platform. For example, ecommerce retailers have far more control over the online shopping experience they offer on their own website than they do on something like Pinterest or Facebook shopping experience (although they can often work together to good effect). Better data, more control over the design, less competition, losing less in commissions – these are just a few of the advantages in having your own presence too.

Your own website is also the ideal place to host a 'subscribe' box, allowing people to sign up to your newsletter, blog (see below), or special offers.

Building an 'opt in' email list is vital in terms of regular contact with people who actually want to hear from you, and gives you some rather clever ways to reach them later on social media too (see our 'Email Marketing' bonus chapter).

If your entire business uses social media and you've no web presence, then you are completely at the mercy of someone else's rules. Your own website, however simple, gives you a space that you truly own and control, that Google will index and, so long as you pay the annual fee to keep the domain name and your hosting, will be there, working for you. It might never be the 'main' platform for your business, and it certainly doesn't need to be expensive or do anything fancy or complicated, but the day might come where you're really glad you have it.

Why you should blog

Your website doesn't have to be the home of your blog, but it would make sense to host it there if you do have one.

And I really think you should blog. I know Gary agrees and we urge participants on our Embrace The Space workshop to write regular blog posts. I hope it's something you'll consider doing.

Everything we're talking about in this book really boils down to increasing awareness of your business by creating quality content. And writing long-form blog posts is perhaps the most effective way to achieve this.

Don't confuse long-form writing with writing hundreds or thousands of words. Blogging doesn't mean writing essays. 'One idea = one blog post' is a good mantra to keep in mind. Try aiming for a few paragraphs and certainly no longer than the equivalent of one page of A4.

The idea is to write quality content, using relevant keywords, which Google will index and deliver to people who use their search engine for particular queries.

'What should I blog about?' is a question many ask. I suggest starting with a list of 12 questions a potential customer might have about your products and services. Or questions which might suggest they need you, even though they don't know it yet.

For example, 'How can I lose weight quickly?' would be a question someone might ask if what they really need was some advice on cooking nutritious, healthy meals or some personal training and fitness advice.

The more specific the question, the better. Write a list of 12 and set about answering one a month. You now have, at a minimum, blog content for a whole year.

Some blogs express opinions too. Your personal take on current events. Your interpretation of how things are just now, your view of the world and how it applies to your business. In his books, Seth Godin makes some powerful analogies about 'tribes' and explains how consumers sometimes choose to spend their money with businesses that they think people like them should be associated with.

For example, if I'm choosing a new car, I'm interested in what a particular model I might buy says about me. What does it mean if I buy a Ferrari? (I wish). Or a Dacia Duster? Or a Porsche? What do these brands and models stand for? At the other extreme, if I'm choosing a professional dog walker for Fido (my imaginary dog – did I mention I'm allergic?), then I might prefer to choose one who has a particular attitude towards our canine friends. And many of us, sometimes consciously or subconsciously, make these decisions day-in, day-out about many aspects of our lives. We consider ourselves part of a 'tribe' and we make choices based around 'what people like me should do'.

Blogging is a great opportunity to win these people over and to set out your mission, vision and values. It's an opportunity to show some depth, take us behind-the-scenes and show us what you stand for.

A restaurant could explain the thinking behind some new additions to their menu; I've used my blog to educate potential customers into the ways the media works and I know Gary has used the NSDesign blog to provide customer service to clients trying to make sense of changes to Google's algorithm.

Committing yourself to regular blogging encourages fresh regular streams of people visiting your website. Google likes it because it values websites which are regularly updated. As a result, your business should become more visible as Google begins to regard you as an authority on the topics you talk about.

Most website builders include blogging elements, if yours doesn't, you could use a dedicated blogging platform such as WordPress, Blogger or Medium, and integrate that with your website or link to it.

Blogging is free; you can have as many blogs as you like and there are very few rules. Some blogs begin as hobbies or side projects and end up as entire businesses themselves. Think Mumsnet and Huffington Post. Others simply provide an opportunity for your 'super-fans' to get to know you a little bit more.

By all means blog for fun. There's a lot of merit in expressing yourself online, the world benefits from more diverse voices sharing ideas and opinions. But if you are doing this for a business, hoping for a business return, then it helps to have some sort of focus on your activity. A blog can be a form of online diary or journal keeping, but taking this literally won't do your business much good. There's an art to connecting the subject matter of your blog post, with the products and services your business offers and the customers who are looking for them. You need a clear purpose. Many successful blogs include a 'call to action': what do you want the reader to do after finishing the blog? Phone you? Download a PDF? Arrange a meeting? It can be anything, but you need to know what it is.

Some of the most engaging social media content often has its roots in blog posts. So, a cafe that specialises in vegan food might write a 500 word blog post on the benefits of a vegan diet, and then share multiple posts across Instagram, Facebook, Twitter and LinkedIn all promoting that blog post, hoping to persuade people to read it in full on their website.

!GeekAlert

WordPress is a website content management system we often recommend. It won't be right for every business, but it's a great starting point, especially if you're new to this and don't have design and coding skills.

Much of WordPress is built around templates and you can have an extremely professional looking site without spending much money or time stressing over it. It's also a very flexible platform (open source) which means when you want to build more complex elements to it, many web designers will be able to work with it, or you might be able to do it yourself via plugins.

There are WordPress plugins that allow you to set up your website so that each time you publish a blog post, your social media profiles are updated automatically, turning your blog into social media content, without any additional work from you.

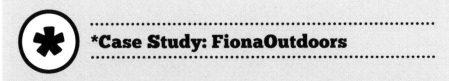

*Case Study: FionaOutdoors

Fiona Russell is a great example of someone who has turned her passion into a blog, and the blog into a business.

Fiona Outdoors – www.fionaoutdoors.co.uk – is a blog that aims to inspire and encourage people to enjoy spending time in the great outdoors, especially in Scotland. The blog draws on personal experiences, activities, recommendations and product reviews, as well as interviews with people and groups.

According to Fiona, the website is her 'guilty pleasure', despite the effort and commitment needed to achieve the levels of success it receives. Blogging for over a decade now, the web statistics are impressive, with just under a quarter of a million annual unique visitors and 35,000 monthly page views, and Fiona's brand is known across the UK and beyond.

She says: "Some people consider me an influencer which is a trendy phrase usually eliciting images of models or celebrities in the gym – and that's certainly not me. When I started the blog, I just wanted to share my experiences with a wide range of people. It was part personal diary and part inspiring others to do things.

"I am aware that people say I motivate or inspire them but to be honest, I'm much more comfortable behind the camera or telling someone else's story. I am trying more and more to showcase what I do and give 'more about me' because other people, especially those in my over-50s age bracket, tell me they are encouraged by what I do. I don't think you will ever see me posing on a mountain in the latest item of fashion wear or whatever. Although, if a top skiing brand wants me to trial their next off-piste skis, please get in touch!"

Aware that a successful blog often depends on achieving the trust of its readers, Fiona is rightly cautious in her approach to monetising the content she produces.

She says: "To earn money directly from a blog you need to accept revenue from sponsored posts or gain income from advertising. I have still not found the right balance for this because sponsored posts and advertising can detract from the purpose of the website, which is to keep people on the site and coming back for more. Few readers enjoy their reading or viewing on a website being interrupted by annoying adverts. I am working on this conundrum, however, and I hope to keep growing the website traffic and, subsequently the earnings.

"I think what I am saying is that what you see me do, or wear, or say is authentic, and I believe it is vital to keep my integrity by remaining independent and honest.

"At the heart of my blog and website is my passion for the outdoors and adventure. As long as that is there, my website will grow and my audience should increase, too. You need to have the passion to keep writing, taking photos and making videos and then you can only hope this brings an income stream, if that is what you are looking for."

CHAPTER IN A TWEET

Despite the huge growth of social media, you absolutely still need a business website. A place YOU control and can make your own, which Google will rank highly (especially if you start blogging) helping link to your social channels, and encouraging email sign-ups.

18

Viral videos

(with some nostalgic advice from a cat)

A joint effort from Gary and Colin

Every Embrace The Space workshop wraps up at the end of the day with a session where we watch some of our favourite viral videos. We've listed them below, along with how they can help your business, and included hyperlinks so you can look them up (tip: use the QR code at the end of the chapter for direct access to all the video links). Give them a watch – you won't be disappointed.

Will It Blend?
Part of a series from Blendtec, an American company that makes, that's right, blenders. This series was one of the first big viral hits just after YouTube launched back in 2006.

In each episode, Blendtec founder Tom Dickson, places an item in a Blendtec blender in order to establish whether or not it is capable of being blended. Over the years items have included half a cooked rotisserie chicken, a camcorder, an Amazon Echo, miniature NFL helmets, Transformers toys and, the episode we show, from April 5th 2010, which features an iPad.

You can watch it here: https://bit.ly/etsbook-willitblend

That single episode has had well over 18 million views, on YouTube alone. The Will It Blend? series has been uploaded to multiple other sites, parodied, remixed and developed a cult following all of its own. There's even a line of merchandise. It's made an unlikely star of Tom Dickson who has appeared on various US chat shows and generated millions of dollars in free publicity for its parent company.

Other companies queue up to give Blendtec free products to trash. What a strange world we live in.

By 1st March 2018, the Will It Blend? series had received a total of 285,005,423 views on YouTube and the campaign continues to this day, some 14 years after it began.

But what about sales? Can a series of daft videos actually sell blenders?

Yes, without a doubt.

Dickson himself commented: "The campaign took off almost instantly. We have definitely felt an impact in sales. Will it Blend? has had an amazing impact on our commercial and our retail products."

In the first year of the campaign, Blendtec achieved a 500% increase in sales (2006 vs 2007), and during that period it cancelled all other paid for forms of advertising and concentrated solely on the YouTube video campaigns.

At its heart, Will It Blend? is an advert but it doesn't look or feel like an advert. The company recognises that blenders are inherently boring and advertising campaigns by other white goods companies do little to entertain or connect with the audience. Blendtec plays up to this. From Dickson's deadpan delivery, to the cheesy music and deliberate low budget production values, viewers perceive Blendtec as an underdog they can champion. The 'fun company' in a boring space. 'The good guys' of the blender world. And as I always say, once you have succeeded in making someone like you, it becomes much easier to sell to them. Often, you won't even have to 'sell', the audience will simply want to buy.

Blendtec succeeds, in fact, every viral video succeeds, because the company understands their audience. They also see themselves as others see them. Blendtec know their product is a bit dull. They know their founder is not a slick sales or marketing guy. But they also know that people who buy blenders, especially younger people buying their first blender, like to be entertained.

They are without doubt, a company which understands our three Golden Rules from Chapter 2 – 'Know the business, Know the customers, and Give them something they want to share'. People couldn't wait for the next video on Blendtec's YouTube channel, and share it (in their millions) they did!

Dollar Shave Club.
More than a great viral video, this is an amazing business idea which netted its founder a fortune.

Mark Levine and Michael Dubin met at a party and discussed the state of male grooming and the price of razor blades. They developed a subscription business that, for a low monthly fee, would deliver high quality razors, direct to your door. And that monthly fee? A dollar.

Here's the video we show:
https://bit.ly/etsbook-dollarshaveclub

Well over 26 million views for this one. And the video was released before the company was properly trading. This was the promotional video to persuade people to register their interest and place pre-orders.

It worked. Within 48 hours more than 100,000 had signed up at the website, pledging to join 'Dollar Shave Club' and the video had been viewed more than eight million times. People share material they find entertaining. With this video, Dollar Shave Club is providing what we call 'social currency', they're giving us something we can pass on to our friends and talk about. In the process, we do their marketing for them.

The video views and the pre-orders attracted the attention of someone else. Big business private equity investors. That video you've just watched convinced investors to back Dollar Shave Club.

Fast forward a few years and we see this cheeky start-up has become a thriving business and a major thorn in the side of the big players in the male grooming sector. Such a thorn in fact, that in 2016, Dollar Shave Club was acquired by Unilever for more than $1 billion.

This video works because it communicates a great idea in a short time. It's just over 90 seconds long and it's packed with entertainment and information. Count the number of times the camera angle changes. Every word in the script matters and is there for a reason. Nothing is wasted. Mike doesn't tell you what age he is, where he studied, or how many years' experience he has in the sector. He's hooked you in straight away. There are other people in the video, an interesting background (that factory isn't his, by the way, he hired it for the day). It helps of course that Mike is a smart, sharp guy and he does have a background in performance and even had some help from a friend with the script.

If you're a dog walking business, local travel agent or small cafè, it's unlikely you'll be able to create something like this, achieve 20 million views and get bought out by Unilever. It might not even make you happy (although I'd quite happily take my chances). But we can all still learn from what makes this work.

1. Ruthless planning.

Every word, every scene, the location, the background, in every shot. The attention to detail is huge in this video.

2. Call to action.

After watching the video, it's obvious what to do next. Visit the website and sign up. Every video should have a very clear purpose, that you can measure.

3. Engaging host.

Mike is the perfect guy to front a video like this. 'Be yourself, with the volume turned up a bit', is a nice rule I heard once when it comes to things like this.

4. Leave nothing to chance.

Even really well produced videos like this don't go viral by accident. Once you have the video and you can see it's generating some traction, that's the ideal time to put a bit of budget behind it and make sure you get it in front of your target audience and influential people who will share it and take your message to a larger audience. You need to find the tipping point: for example, could a celebrity share this on their own social media channels or might it be featured in the mainstream media?

Many videos have caught our eye over the years and been featured in our workshops. Not just because they were fun and made us laugh (which most of them did), but because there are clear business lessons to be learned in all of them, about how to engage an audience, and be memorable for all the right reasons.

Here's a quick look back at some other favourites.

The T-Mobile Royal Wedding:
https://bit.ly/etsbook-tmobilewedding

Old Spice – The Man Your Man Could Smell like[93]:
https://bit.ly/etsbook-oldspice

KLM Surprise (as featured in our Classic case studies):
https://bit.ly/etsbook-klmsurprise

Tea Consent:
https://bit.ly/etsbook-teaconsent

Advice from a cat

Time for a quick one as we finish this chapter in the same way we currently close all our full day Embrace The Space workshops. Throughout the course, Gary makes frequent references to 'social media is about more than just cat videos'. The truth is, he's easily entertained and happens to own a cat so he's sympathetic to the concept. I on the other hand, am allergic to cats. But I still enjoy this next video. It is a cat video, but unlike any you'll have seen before[94].

Charley Says: https://bit.ly/etsbook-charleyvideo

A nice lesson there for anyone contemplating sending a Tweet. We'd probably all do well to heed that advice sometimes.

There's a reason why we mention 'cat videos' throughout the workshop and it all comes back to understanding your audience. The fact is the people whose attention you are trying to attract, your followers on social media, are not there hanging on your every word.

Nobody ever joined Twitter, Facebook, Instagram, YouTube, Pinterest or

---

[93] This one was actually on the TV again just recently! 20 years on from its YouTube success it's still working for the company on mainstream media.

[94] If you're as old as Gary is, you'll maybe remember the 'real' Charley the cat from your childhood memories. Here's a wee reminder: https://bit.ly/etsbook-charleysays

LinkedIn because they are interested in YOU. They joined those networks, primarily to be entertained and in some cases, to be informed.

When the average social media user browses their news feed, they are not thinking about you and your business. They're thinking about news, their family, friends, sport, the weather, celebrities, archive pictures of where they live, that cafè they visited on holiday last summer and so it goes on. And for some, they will sit for extended periods of time and watch videos of cats.

There's nothing you or I can do to change that. That's how a huge section of the population uses social media. The challenge then is to say something about you and your business that connects with them. That makes them stop, pay attention and choose to watch your video and then, having done so, decide to share it with their friends and family and the rest of their network.

Think about that for a moment. Success with your video on social media means that the viewers watch it and then risk their own reputation by passing it on to their own followers. That's quite a big ask.

I hope you have come to understand that the traditional 'corporate video' will not cut it in this social media world. It's not as simple as having the marketing team approve a carefully worded script and hiring a film crew to come in for the day to show your business off in a glossy production.

One thing all the videos we show have in common is they're cheap. And they're also down to earth and real, but a lot of thought has gone into them.

It's the authenticity that makes the difference and the connection created between your business and the audience. Video, when done well, is a great way to establish a genuine connection.

These well-known 'viral videos' are, of course, the ultimate examples. The 1% that achieve millions of views.

But there's much more to video than going viral. In fact, in our training we advise against setting out to try and achieve a viral video. Instead, it's better to concentrate on making video part of an on-going, regular dialogue. Short, behind-the-scenes clips for Instagram stories or Twitter. Video testimonials from happy customers placed throughout your website. Maybe even short 'teasers' explaining how you work with clients or showing your creative process.

Every major social network now accepts (some would say 'craves') video content and wants you to produce more of it. Many audiences would prefer to watch a video than to read copy. And if you uploaded video content direct to your social network of choice, you will often achieve a much higher reach than if you'd posted plain text or a link to a video elsewhere.

So, think 'video first', build a real connection with your audience and reap the rewards.

*Case Study: Alexander's Family Butchers

I think it's fair to say the first time I met Jim and Donna Alexander at their butcher's premises in Darvel, Ayrshire, they were incredibly frustrated with their business. A lack of footfall was the main issue; people just weren't coming through the doors in sufficient numbers to make the business viable.

Like so many small business owners, Jim and Donna had poured their heart and soul into the business. Jim was a highly skilled, experienced butcher who had been in the trade since he was 16 years old. Eighteen months before I met him, he had decided to fulfil his dream and take over the butcher's in Darvel, delivering a hybrid approach between physical retail from the shop and online orders.

After some initial encouragement (anything 'new' in Darvel is guaranteed a certain level of attention!), a downward trend in sales began, leaving Jim and Donna facing an inevitable decision. Grasping for optimism, I asked how the online side of things was going. There seemed to be some hope there but not enough to compensate for the lack of sales through the shop. However, the more I spoke with Jim and Donna, the more I realised they were willing to 'try anything!' to turn things around.

I could see that Jim was quite a personality. We got chatting about meat-eating and the debate (which was raging at the time) about whether it was 'bad' and should we all be turning vegan. He gave such passionate, thoughtful responses, I began to realise he was exactly the sort of individual who could engage an audience. I was reminded of a guy I'd seen with a stall at Stables Market in Camden, London, who sits all day live streaming himself creating jigsaws. If no-one was coming into the butcher's shop, perhaps sending Jim 'out' to people could drive interest in the business. Video was the obvious way to do it.

We devised a strategy with two main pillars: firstly, instructional content where Jim would showcase his skills and expertise, demonstrating how to make affordable meals with his products, and explaining the benefits of shopping with a dedicated butcher. Secondly, (and my back-up plan), was to attempt to make Jim a 'star'! My thinking was that if the business failed, Jim would have social content he could be proud of and a profile which might help if he had to look for a new job.

When you do as much training and consultancy as I do, you learn early on how to spot the businesses which will actually put into practice what they've spent a few hours talking about. I knew Jim and Donna were dedicated, but even I wasn't expecting them to set about things with such commitment. They'd published a post before I'd even arrived back in my office and kept it going, daily, as I'd suggested for several weeks. The reach on their Facebook page grew and a community began interacting with Jim. There was no sign whatsoever of a corresponding increase in sales, but a dialogue was opening up.

Fast forward a couple of months, and after continued regular social content from Jim and Donna, they decided to ask their Facebook audience some honest questions: 'What would it take for you to shop with us?', 'What do you think our opening hours should be?', 'If we opened late on a Wednesday and opened earlier on a Saturday morning, would you be more likely to shop here?'

The response from the Facebook audience was really encouraging and the insights achieved, and the changes Jim and Donna made to the business as a result, did lead to real progress. Through social media Jim and Donna gained greater understanding of their customers' needs. Market research worth its weight in gold.

The success of their social media adventure rekindled the love Jim and Donna had for their business, and proved it was viable, just not in Darvel. So they relocated to an industrial unit in Kilmarnock which allowed them to work with larger quantities of meat and operate a trade counter, selling to customers who had placed orders online.

Things got off to a good start and then, out of the blue, came the COVID-19 lockdown and panic buying in supermarkets. Suddenly, Jim had a queue.

A long queue. Scores of new customers. The entire family was roped in managing the orders and helping with deliveries. Some very long days and nights were required. But throughout it all, the Alexander's Family Butchers Facebook page kept a dialogue going with their customers, updating them on the status of their orders and deliveries, opening hours, social distancing rules and what products were available and when. It was transformative. They generated much goodwill, and a significant proportion of the new customers the business acquired during the lockdown look likely to continue to shop with them for the long term, either face to face or via their website which is experiencing great success.

Social media can help you tackle adversity. It doesn't always need to be about trumpeting success; you can use the platforms to generate interest by being human, and talking to your customers about what matters to you and them.

CHAPTER IN A TWEET

Don't set out to create a 'viral' video. Regular, simple videos of you, at work, sharing what you know to be authentic and true, will engage the right people and deliver value to your business, sometimes in ways you might not expect. And if it goes viral - result!

19

Before you go: Dinosaur or Dodo?

(Probably neither because you're reading this)

Gary

Time for a quick history lesson.

Approximately 66 million years ago, 75% of all plant and animal life on the rock that we now call Earth was wiped out when a slightly smaller rock crashed into it. The Cretaceous–Paleogene (K–Pg) extinction event as it's now known[95] is what most scientific boffins believe caused the final extinction of the dinosaurs. I repeat, in simple terms – a huge rock, out of nowhere, fell on them. They had no idea it was coming, they could do nothing about it[96], and after the dust had settled, the dinosaurs were all dead.

Fast forward to the late 16th century, and to the island of Mauritius, east of Madagascar in the Indian Ocean. The Dodo – a flightless bird resembling a large gormless pigeon – had been an inhabitant here for possibly many 100's of years, and other than some occasional bickering between the Dodo clans, had lived a peaceful, if somewhat uneventful, existence.

But as tends to happen, things changed, and over the next few decades they were slowly but surely joined on the island by other animals, including the two-legged ones we call humans. Being the playful, curious and trusting creatures that they were (some might say stupid, ignorant, and naive), the Dodos welcomed these newcomers with open arms[97], despite the fact that humans were undermining their very existence.

I repeat, in simple terms – the Dodos surely were aware that their environment was changing. New circumstances were clearly threatening them and yet they didn't seem to react to what was happening; they didn't run away and they didn't (or couldn't) adapt. Eventually the Dodos were gone; extinct, not through the fault of some random chance event, but because they failed to react to what was happening all around them. Things happened quickly and they just didn't evolve at the necessary pace, so they paid the ultimate price.

You might be surprised (or you might not be) that still today, on a weekly basis, I hear my favourite 'I'm a bit of a dinosaur' excuse from business owners as they explain why they don't engage with social media, or embrace

---

[95] Obviously I knew this, and didn't rely on Wikipedia to make me look intellectual.
[96] None of them had Bruce Willis's phone number.
[97] Metaphorical of course.

technology, or have a website. They normally laugh when they tell me this, and genuinely think it's ok to blame their age, or attitude to technology as the reason why they choose not to adapt or change. If this is you, here's the reality: YOU ARE NOT A DINOSAUR. YOU ARE A DODO.

Stop doing the dinosaurs a disservice. They were actually at the peak of their game, the head of the food chain, the rulers of the earth. It wasn't their fault they were wiped out; it was that freak incident with a meteor.

Dodos on the other hand......they just didn't react. Island life had been comfortable and they were fixed in their behaviour. So on they went, regardless of the dangers. Maybe they thought, 'It'll be fine'.

Social media is not a new thing. It didn't just come out of nowhere, and there's no excuse for not realising the impact of digital disruption. Business giants across all sectors have rued not embracing technological change, and there's enough evidence right in front of you to see the (often not so slow) implications of choosing (because that's what it is, a choice) not to evolve.

> **66** The one path that never works is the most
> common one: doing nothing at all. **99**
> **Seth Godin, Tribes**

So whether you're a dinosaur or a dodo, the fact is, you're not relevant. Not relevant because you choose to ignore Facebook as a route to market. Not relevant because you choose to demand that your customers call your annoying nine-to-five telephone line. Not relevant because you think making videos on YouTube is pointless, and 'nobody else in our industry does that'. Not relevant because you ban mobile phones in the workplace, or block Instagram via the company firewall. I could keep going with more examples, but I think you get the point.

The good news is you are relevant. You are neither Dinosaur nor Dodo. At the very least you're on the right journey, and embracing change (as scary as it can often be) is something you realise is vital to your organisation's success and future existence.

How do I know this? Because you've now completed reading this book.

And on behalf of Colin and myself – thank you for doing so. But reading a book is easy. Attending a workshop is easy. Knowing you need to make changes is easy. Actually making them? Don't stop now, and give us a shout if we can help.

CHAPTER IN A TWEET

There's really no excuse for ignoring the impact of social media on today's modern business world. The whole 'I'm a dinosaur' doesn't cut it any more. Not embracing social media is a choice, and if that's you, then you're not a dinosaur, you're a dodo. Good luck.

Bonus Chapters

OK, so we lied... you've not quite finished the book just yet. If you want to, you can put it back on the shelf, consider it done, and start on one of those other books that you got three Christmases ago and haven't yet got round to reading. We won't take offence.

Or you can revel in the fact that we've written you some bonus chapters!

Why bonus chapters? Why not just include them as normal chapters, and then you'd actually know when the end of the book is?

Well, like any good Bon Jovi concert, there's always an encore when Jon and the boys finish up with a few songs you didn't expect (usually Beatles covers), but which add the final touches to your night. With Bon Jovi it's actually in the second encore when this usually happens, the first being used to sing 'Always' followed by 'Livin' on a Prayer'[98].

These bonus chapters cover topics that aren't specifically related to our main topic of Social Media, but which are almost impossible not to consider when 'doing' social media. The advice given in the chapters that follow nearly always makes an appearance in some shape or form in the many workshops we run, and in the 1-2-1 consultancies we deliver. While each subject probably merits its own book, we didn't want to conclude this book without at least mentioning them, and giving you a little bit of 'Twist and Shout' before the final curtain.

SCAN ME FOR BONUS
CHAPTER RESOURCES

---

[98] Colin just hit me, and told me I was "off on a bloody Bon Jovi tangent again" so I'll get back to the point.

Bonus Mini-Chapter

Search Engine Optimisation (SEO)

Gary

While SEO arguably merits more than just a few paragraphs (if not a whole book), I'd like to pass on just a few words of wisdom with regard to this important topic, and suggest some ways in which it overlaps with social media.

Firstly, what is SEO and why is it important for business owners to understand at least the basics?

SEO – Search Engine Optimisation – simply means the practice of optimising (typically) a website so that Google[99] ranks it higher in its search results than other websites. A higher ranking usually results in more people visiting that website[100].

And let's be frank here, it's mainly websites that Google wants to return. Not social media platforms. So to recap Chapter 17, yes, you still need a website, as that's how a huge chunk of your future customers are going to discover you in the first place, because they Googled something, and ended up on your website. From there, I might now discover your Facebook or Instagram, but rarely do I click straight there from Google.

Two very important things I'd like to stress when it comes to SEO:

1. There's no such thing as the 'top of Google'. It means nothing. What does matter is being 'top of Google' for something specific; for example, it's important that the NSDesign website appears at (or near to) the top of the results when someone searches for 'Social Media Training'. Somewhat less important is that we rank highly for 'John Cena vs the Rock'[101]. Be careful of anyone promising you 'top of Google', and if you must entertain such promises of success, always make sure you know what keywords (explained soon) they are basing these promises on. Pay me £50 and I'll 100% guarantee you the first spot on Google (for a phrase no one ever searches for).

2. 'Top of Google' is different for everyone. The world's most popular search engine is now personalised more than ever before. My results

---

[99] Other Search Engines are available, but given Google has over 85% of the search market, who cares.
[100] Bad joke alert: Where's the best place to hide a dead body? Page two of Google.
[101] Randomly we got 23 visitors to our site who searched for this last year! This is entirely Colin's fault as he blogged about this topic on the website back in 2011.

are different to Colin's results which are different to your results. So just because you see your own website in the number one spot when you search for an important phrase, doesn't mean everyone does. Many times I have made people cry[102] when I prove that their claims of 'I'm already top' are purely based on their own checking. Google knows it's you. It knows you're always on your own website. It prioritises your site (among others) more for you than others. At the very least, when trying to check your own site's ranking, make sure you log-out of Google. Maybe also clear your cache, reboot your router, and browse using the 'incognito' mode. If you really want to test things impartially, then drive 300 miles away from your office, visit a public library[103], and search from there. Even then it won't be what everyone else sees, but at least it's getting closer to it, and you enjoyed some nice scenery on the journey.

It's all about the keywords

At the risk of playing down the importance of SEO and belittling every book, or full day workshop on the topic (many of which I've delivered over the years!), the basics are actually pretty straight forward. Despite what some SEO experts might want you to believe, it really isn't rocket science, and comes down to you asking one simple question: 'Is my website about the thing they are searching for?'.

Are the keywords the person has used (that is, the words/phrase typed into the search engine box), featured on your website? Do you talk about those things? Are the words mentioned? More than once? In the right places? What about synonyms of those words?

The biggest mistake business owners make is that they use the wrong words. Their website homepage is full of words and phrases understood by business owners (not customers), with jargon and acronyms used by the industry, or marketing nonsense which doesn't actually help people find the site in the first place.

---

[102] Rarely do they actually cry, but there have been a few awkward exceptions.
[103] I recommend Orkney Library (for many reasons).

If you're a web design company based in Kilmarnock, and your homepage says that you're 'proud to have been creating beautiful digital experiences for 30 years, helping global clients connect with their customers based on intuitive UX digital strategies and best practice UI touch points, creating mixed media portals helping improve ROI through understanding of user journeys', then it might make you sound fancy and better than all those other web design companies out there, but it doesn't actually help you get found by potential customers searching for 'web design Ayrshire'[104]. Since you failed to mention that.

Now of course, what you don't do is go in the opposite direction. You don't force the keywords into every available inch of website content. 'Hi, we're a web design company based in Ayrshire, and if you need web design in Ayrshire, then we're in Ayrshire and do web design. If web design is what you need, come to Ayrshire's best web design company and get your web design from us. In Ayrshire.' Known as Keyword Spamming, Google will see what you're up to, and you're only going in one direction in the rankings – down.

But creating a website using the right words, with a bit of volume (density), written in a clear, understandable manner – and you're halfway there[105], helping Google to return your website to customers who might actually be a good fit for you.

!GeekAlert

Check out some of these powerful (but simple) tools to help you better understand what people actually search for. (You'll be able to work out the websites for these – just Google them!):

> **Google Trends**
> **Answer the Public**
> **UberSuggest**

---

[104] At the time of writing, the phrase 'web design Ayrshire' had been searched for over 1000 times on Google in the previous 30 days.
[105] Complete the Bon Jovi lyrics.

Note that there's way more to SEO than what we've covered here, but start with your content, and think like a customer. What are they looking for? What words do they use? What do they call it? Thinking in these terms doesn't just help your website or blog get found in Google, it helps your business get found period.

People 'search' every day on multiple platforms. On Facebook, on Amazon, on Twitter, on YouTube. Applying the same thinking to every bit of content you produce will help more people find you, and if I find you, I might like what you're saying, begin to trust you, and maybe (just maybe) become a customer. If I don't find you in the first place, then.....sorry – who are you?

Bonus Mini-Chapter

Podcasting

Colin

As a former award winning national radio broadcaster (have I mentioned that yet?!) podcasting is, unsurprisingly, something I enjoy very much. They are quick and simple to produce and can be so easily distributed around the world. They are low cost, and anyone can share opinions, ideas and advice, in a matter of minutes. Just as some people will tell you 'everyone's got a book in them', I genuinely believe, every individual, and every business, is capable of producing a good podcast.

You can do it as a marketing activity for your business (and that's our main focus here) but if there's a particular subject, cause or hobby you are passionate about, then creating your own, might just become one of the best things you've ever done.

Podcasting is hot right now. It's big business. Every organisation has a story to tell and podcasting is a really powerful way to set out what you stand for, to take me behind-the-scenes and build casual audiences into passionate advocates for your brand.

Importance of purpose

How do you do it? First, you need something to say. A reason, and a purpose and an underlying business objective. Why are you doing this? What do you want this podcast to achieve? Is it direct sales? Leads generation? People coming to visit you at the trade show? Maybe you're hoping to start a discussion or build a reputation as an expert. There's no right or wrong here, you just need to know what you hope to achieve with it.

Next, decide on the format for your podcast. What is it? 20 minutes once a month? You and a colleague discussing the burning issues of the day? A full-on well produced documentary? Is it funny? Serious? How will it be different from the podcasts already out there dealing with that same subject matter? Why should anyone listen to you?

That might take some significant time and discussion. When you've sorted it out, be honest about what you can commit to. How often will you publish? Realistically, what is achievable? Weekly? Monthly? Less often than that? It'll help you in the long run if you can set reasonable expectations and commit to some sort of schedule. I advise launching with three or four episodes uploaded at once and committing to a series of maybe six or eight episodes. Complete the series and then you can take a break, evaluate it and if things have gone well you can return for a second series. Don't just let things fizzle out and don't end up like some businesses that started a blog and published two posts in 2013, added another in 2015 then lost the password and to this day have a 'Blog' section on their website that really doesn't show them in a very good light.

Podcasting technicalities

Podcasts are different to MP3 or WAV audio files sitting on a website. A 'proper' podcast has a hosting provider, has distribution to major podcast platforms and directories such as Apple Podcasts, Spotify, iHeartRadio, Google and TuneIn. There are certain 'best practice' guidelines in terms of audio quality, bit rate and the artwork that accompanies your podcast. None of this is particularly challenging, it just requires a bit of set up. Choose the right hosting provider (Libysn, Podbean and Podomatic are good places to start) and they'll keep you right and take you through this all step by step. Once it's in place, any podcast you upload is immediately distributed to audiences everywhere, on whichever platform they prefer. You can also grab links and share individual episodes through your social media channels or embed it all on your website.

Don't forget about smart speakers, like the Amazon Echo, which continue to grow in popularity. Your podcast could appear there too.

'Podcasting is free' is a nice slogan but isn't entirely true. But I do believe publishing one is accessible to everyone. Expect to pay around £15+VAT a month for a decent hosting plan but you could certainly record on your existing smartphone. It might not be the best option, especially if you are looking to add additional elements such as music or multiple tracks, and if you have a lot of editing to do, you might find that easier to do on a laptop or desktop. But a couple of clip on microphones, maybe a semi-pro USB mic as well, free editing software such as Audacity, some royalty free theme music, and maybe a Zoom account to record interviews with remote guests, and you could put everything together for less than a couple of hundred pounds. If you do publish one, let me know, so I can give it a listen. And if you don't do your own, perhaps you'll find one you can appear on as a guest.

We're often told that audiences these days have short attention spans and every piece of content we create should be as short and snappy as we can make it. That's true and it's a good discipline to get into. But at the same time, these same audiences are also increasingly enjoying content with some substance. Something more laid back, in-depth and longer form. Something to listen to on the commute, something they can learn from, something interesting, something that brings about change. I think there's an opportunity there for you.

Bonus Mini-Chapter

Email marketing

Gary

Despite what some social media experts claim, email marketing is not dead. Social media hasn't killed email. Huge volumes of spam haven't killed email, and neither has GDPR. It's actually still alive and well, and should definitely be considered as part of your digital marketing tool box.

Almost everyone has an email account (don't believe the hype – youths too!), and most people check it every day. Being able to reach the inbox of your customer (or prospective customer) allows a direct 1-2-1 message which when done well, can achieve high conversion rates and build better relationships. Done badly, you're just an annoying spammer and with 'one click' I'll not be bothered by you again.

It's maybe not quite as sexy a topic as Instagram, or Tiktok, but email marketing can play a vital role in helping your business achieve results, and it comes down to one thing. Permission.

Let's get the legal stuff out the way

Unlike some other areas of digital marketing, what you can and cannot do with email with regard to marketing a business is pretty clear cut.

In 2018 the General Data Protection Regulation (or GDPR[106]) came into force. Among its many requirements, is a need for businesses to have a 'legal basis' for collecting, storing, and using personal data, i.e. any piece of data that, used alone or with other data, could identify a person. As such, most email addresses (those of your customers, staff, stakeholders etc.) typically fall under this banner.

While there are many 'legal bases' you could consider, the simple one which I suggest you aim for is CONSENT. You need permission. Permission to collect and store an email in the first place. Permission to then use it and send that person an email which they are willing to receive. Permission to use that email address elsewhere for other purposes. You either have permission, or you don't.

---

[106] Lovingly often called the 'God Damn Privacy Rules'.

And if you have it, how do you prove it? Because if a complaint is lodged with the Information Commissioner's Office (ICO) that you spammed someone (i.e. emailed them something of a 'commercial nature' without consent), then you'll need to prove otherwise, or risk a fine, damage to your reputation, or both.

Just because they consent, do they actually want it?

Yes, you should use your GDPR legal requirements to clean up your lists[107], but the real reason to do it, and ensure you have permission from people before you email them, is why would you even want to email someone who doesn't want your messages? Why haven't you been taking this approach for years? What's the point in having people in a list that, while they haven't yet complained about you, hardly benefit the business as they politely delete every email that comes in without ever getting past the headline.

With actual real consent, comes a degree of desire. I wouldn't have bothered consenting if I didn't actually want to receive your email. And if I want it, I might read it, and if I read it.....you get the point.

Think about the email newsletters and marketing alerts you receive yourself. Which ones do you actively read and why? And which ones make their way to the trash folder. Often without you even realising why (you probably just got bored, or fed up with what the sender was communicating).

Now's the time to stop all those old 'email everyone in the list' tactics, and start applying some of the best practices we've already introduced to you.

Remember the 'Give them something they want to share' advice (Golden Rule number three from Chapter 2). What about the 'niche content for niche audiences' best practice (given in our 'Paid Social' advice in Chapter 8). And finally, all that advice we gave about good content in Chapter 6.

---

[107] See our approach: https://bit.ly/etsbook-gdprlists

Why do so many businesses see email permission as a license to ignore every bit of content best practice, and turn into a spammer? 'It's ok, we can send them this, they ticked the box'. Rather than consider what the customer would actually like to receive from you.

Don't just fall into the obvious email content such as 'newsletters' (many businesses make up stuff to merit sending a newsletter!) or 'special offers' (especially if it's not actually special in any way) but consider email as another route to share value, in a similar way to how we hope you're using your social platforms.

Allow people to subscribe to your Blog, and have these sent via email as soon as you write one. If you know your industry inside out, then share links and sector news to others who want the same. You might even want to carry out some customer research, or send regular FAQs.[108]

Building the list in the first place

So how do you (legally) build an email list in the first place? If you haven't already started this, do it now. The quicker you start building it, the quicker you can use it. And make your life easier by employing one of the many (often free) email campaign management tools, which not only help you design and send out the emails later on, but help build (and maintain) a clean list in the first place.

Mailchimp.com and CampaignMonitor.com are two of the most commonly used systems for small and medium sized businesses, and among their many features they help with the 'subscribe code' for your website (yes, that thing you still need which we explained earlier!).

Best practice is to consider some aspect of list segmentation; the ability to choose who receives your email based on things like location, interest, or where they are on the user journey. Emails which are 'sent to everyone'

---

[108] FAQs = Frequently asked questions. Although there is a train of thought which says if a question is frequently asked, you've not been explaining it well enough elsewhere.

always under-perform compared to emails containing content where you've been specific about who it's best suited to.

A joined up approach

One of the best things about having a permission based email list is being able to use it for things other than email! Yes, you could simply email everyone, but (on the assumption you received consent) you could also use it to show subscribers an advert on Facebook, LinkedIn or Twitter.

Called 'Remarketing' this is the ability to communicate with a social media user through having their email address, and showing them paid adverts on the platform of your choice.

For example: a hotel showing only existing customers (from the last two years) an advert for discounted rooms once lockdown restrictions are removed. These people already know you. They're further down the customer journey, so you wouldn't need to educate them on who you are, or why they should stay. They've been before, so just convince them to come again with the deal.

Get consent, get growing your list, and start getting clever about how to use what is a hugely valuable, always under-rated asset – the humble email address.

Bonus Mini-Chapter

Social in the real world

Gary and Colin

Way back in Chapter 2 we reminded you of the importance of truly understanding your audience. The actual people that you want to connect with, develop some rapport, and influence. Real people with real lives which extend beyond their mobile phones and computer screens.

Far too often we've seen businesses place social media and other digital activity in a silo, separate to everything else they're doing in the physical world, and treating online and offline customers as different target markets.

If you're lucky enough to have an actual physical touch-point with customers, then clever (often simple) integration of your social media into these spaces might be a good route to increasing online business. Try some of these online/offline crossover strategies:

Put your URLs on any physical asset you have.

If you have any sort of physical premises (a shop, an office, exterior signage, delivery vans etc.) make sure it includes your website address. As we've discussed, your website brings together all your social media and acts as your official online home, so take every opportunity to remind people of how to get there. Your physical location likely presents a huge opportunity: think of the number of people that walk past it every day, who look into your window, or see your branded vehicles. Take the opportunity to tell them how to find you online. Some businesses even integrate their domain name into the actual business name, e.g. sportsdirect.com or jdsports.co.uk, and put that in huge letters above their door.

Could you use QR codes?

I'll never forget the excited look on Gary's face as he told me his new toaster had a QR code on the back of it. When he scanned the code with his phone it took him to an instructional video. WHAT KIND OF INDIVIDUAL NEEDS INSTRUCTIONS TO OPERATE A TOASTER???!! (This is what I have to work with). Anyway, perhaps for more complex activities this is a great idea. It reduces the need to physically print things that often get lost and has a huge variety of potential uses.

QR codes are free to create and can be used to take people to any website, social media platform or to trigger many other actions, such as sending a text message or downloading a file. I've seen them on For Sale signs (to download schedules of homes for sale), petrol pumps and restaurant menus (to make it easy to pay), on billboard adverts and even in books (as additional content or to keep things up to date between editions[109]). One local ice cream shop we worked with used a QR code – printed boldly on the exterior wall – effectively to increase their Facebook likes from people waiting in summer queues, by promising a free extra topping on their ice cream for customers who 'scan and like'. Another client in the construction industry had their code custom printed on every manager's high-vis safety jacket, which when scanned took you to their LinkedIn profile!

!GeekAlert

QR Codes are more popular than ever before, and despite having existed for over 20 years, the fact that most modern smartphones no longer even need a separate app (you just scan them with the camera) means they are seeing a resurgence in creative usage.

Consider them a bridge between offline and online, and think how you might take advantage of them.

You can create your own free QR code here https://bit.ly/etsbook-qrcodes

Most of the social platforms now incorporate QR codes in some shape or form, with Facebook allowing you to easily create them for things like events[110] and Twitter using them to help you gain more followers. WhatsApp recently launched QR codes to facilitate swapping details, removing the obstacle of manually entering a phone number into the app before connecting with a friend or business. Adding a QR code to a receipt or in your shop window now allows you to provide immediate support or sales assistance to your customers on a platform they're already using to talk to their friends.

---

[109] Only cutting edge authors consider doing this.
[110] And at the time of writing is investigating how it might use them to facilitate payments.

Or a physical 'Likes' counter?

We'd like to assume that if you run a retail shop of any sort, that on the front door you've stuck up a 'Like us on Facebook' sticker (which Facebook used to officially give out, but now you have to make your own[111]). It's a simple friendly reminder to customers that you're on Facebook, and simply because it exists, and they see it, means you'll no doubt pick up a few extra likes after (or even during) their visit, keen to connect with you for future special offers or follow on customer service.

How about upping your game and adding a Facebook 'Likes' counter?

Take a fish and chip shop, ice cream van, car garage waiting room – anywhere people typically queue or wait for assistance. Put a counter from https://www.smiirl.com in a prominent position and watch your customers' faces light up as they 'like' you on your social media channel of choice and the numbers on the counter spin round.

The numbers physically spin the moment you click 'like' on the Facebook (or Instagram) app! The customer has just (by tapping their screen) made the real world change, right in front of their eyes![112]

Some businesses even put a sign beside the counter offering a low cost incentive, e.g. 'free pickled onion', in exchange for a 'like'. People will do it just to see if it works; although the danger is they click again to 'unlike' you and watch the numbers go backwards!

Embrace the #selfie generation!

While you might not be as keen as Gary is to take endless selfies and share them on Instagram, understand that he's not alone. Like them or loathe them, selfies (and other forms of 'User Generated Content') are on the increase, with the general public's love to share anything and everything (especially pictures of themselves) a huge opportunity for your business.

---

[111] Yet another reason why every business owner needs a laminator.
[112] Gary wrote this part, and I fear he's more excitable than most people waiting in queues.

As we covered in Chapter 10, when 'the people become your marketing', it's a very powerful message. So an amazing Facebook photo from my best friend staying at your boutique hotel might be more influential than any image you can show me. Or an Instagram Story from my co-worker with your beautifully painted feature wall in the background (coincidentally perfectly sized for a selfie) might have me wanting to book a meal at the weekend.

Don't just hope they happen – pro-actively design your physical spaces to encourage them. From simple 'selfie boards' situated at relevant points in your premises (a tactic we've seen work for businesses from trampoline parks to kitchen showrooms) to carefully curated selfie hotspots, designed to give your visitor the ultimate backdrop for their next social share. An image is worth a thousand words, so let your audiences say amazing things about you by showcasing your business to the best.

Whatever you do, don't blame the internet

It's not the digital world's fault for any downturn in 'real world' business. Don't be one of those retailers who complains that the internet is killing them, yet does nothing to attempt to trade online. Don't be dismissive of having a website because your type of product isn't sold online (how do you think they're finding you in the first place?). And don't be a tourist attraction that bans taking #selfies because you think it's crass and not befitting of your stature (when all the world wants to do is share amazing photos with their friends).

Embrace the offline/online crossover, and look to enhance your real world experience, with online benefits. A physical shop on the high street with QR Codes linking to online shopping or customer reviews. A family law specialist with a website and blog optimised for the keywords related to what soon-to-be divorcees type into Google. Or the historic castle that encourages photos from the best corner of the garden, showcasing the attraction across social media with a branded hashtag to boot!

We love working with physical businesses to introduce some aspect of digital transformation to help them evolve and thrive in today's business landscape; so if this is something you would like to discuss further with Gary or myself, get in touch to see how we can help.

#TrainerLife

Passion, performance and purpose

··

My kids will often ask me: 'Don't you get bored always telling people the same thing?'.

I completely understand why they might think that. They see me running yet another workshop, or another webinar, on the topic of Social Media Strategy, or Facebook, or Instagram etc. They see me preparing for another Embrace The Space masterclass, packing up the car with the selfie boards, printing some of the group activities, and making changes to the relevant presentations. They see it as every other kid would – it's Dad's job, and on the face of it, it looks very repetitive, dull and boring.

The truth is, it's anything but.

Every day is different, and while the topics might be the same (I once delivered the same three hour Facebook workshop, three times back to back in different parts of the country), the audience is always different.....And so in every session, I engage in different chat, advice, banter, discussion, tangents, lessons learned (on both sides), surprises and fun.

And of course the subject matter does change. Social media is one of the most exciting, fast paced, dynamic sectors to work in. The landscape is always moving, and the platforms are regularly rolling out new features, or entirely new social networks are emerging out of nowhere. I always jokingly say to attendees that 'we're immersed in all this geeky stuff on a daily basis so you don't need to be'. It really is a full time job just keeping up with everything!

While standing in front of a room of 50 business owners (or presenting to them via webcam) might not be for everyone, for me it's as close as I'll get to performing at Hampden with Bon Jovi[113]. It's exciting, it's

---

[113] Not quite the same, but I did once perform with the boyband 5ive on stage at the Fiddlers nightclub in Largs, and to quote the Sun newspaper (clearly a slow news day) I totally 'owned it'! Feel free to Google it.

exhilarating, it's a chance to show off my inner-geek, and share my passion of all things digital with my other passion of 'teaching it'.

I've been on enough training workshops to know that some trainers do indeed look bored. They look like they've told the same scripted story a thousand times, and present to the audience in a 'death by PowerPoint'[114] style, reading bullet points word for word, conveying anything but passion or enthusiasm for their topic. I won't lie, it's one of my bugbears, and I'll often have a moan about uninspiring speakers[115] and their lack of effort to enthuse an audience, or to make training sessions fun and enjoyable[116]. Learning anything is so much easier when you're enjoying the experience, and that's arguably one of the most important jobs of a trainer.

And so I'll finish this final #TrainerLife anecdote with advice from Jon Bon Jovi which by his own admission he pinched from Mick Jagger (I think he shared this story during an interview with Oprah years ago: I've since looked for this clip on YouTube and can't find it, but it did happen, and I'm not just making this up!). When asked how he maintained his consistent energy during every single performance over his 30 year career (whether performing to 50 or to 50,000) he simply said:

> **❝** Perform every show with the passion, enthusiasm, excitement and energy as if it was the very first one. For the audience it most likely is. **❞**

Nobody deserves a less than 100% performance, especially if they're paying you for it. Whether you're selling burgers, engineering consultancy, or first aid training[117], giving the customer the best possible experience is, in my opinion, one of the core responsibilities of a business. You might not be having the best day, but your customers need to see you 'being great' regardless.

---

[114] For the record, the issue is never PowerPoint. It's always the trainer using it.
[115] https://bit.ly/etsbook-shitspeakers
[116] https://bit.ly/etsbook-funlearning
[117] I know someone who sells all three. True.

If it ever comes to the point where we're not seeing words like inspiring, energetic, passionate, fun, exciting, brilliant, and 'wow' on the evaluation and feedback forms submitted after our workshops, then that's when I'll hang up my trainer boots.

I encourage everyone reading this to find your purpose, find your voice, and share it with passion. That way everyone wins.

Gary

The End

Ok. No lies this time. We really are done. Unless of course you want to continue turning the pages and read a little more about the people behind this book. But if you don't, that's fine – we won't hold it against you.

About the authors

and the illustrator

More about Colin (as written by Gary).

Colin Kelly has a voice for radio. Some would say a face for it too. He's been my partner in crime delivering the Embrace The Space social media masterclass for over a decade now, and there's no one else I'd rather present alongside[118].

In the past we've been called the 'Ant and Dec' of the training world[119], with Colin obviously playing the quirky Anthony McPartlan role to my smooth talking Declan Donnelly (although our heights would maybe swap round for that comparison[120]), but joking aside, just like the cheeky chappies from the telly, it's our on-stage relationship that make our workshops special.

Before we worked together, I used Colin as a case study. A popular DJ at the time, Colin was one of the first in that business to use Twitter – not just for promotion or marketing, but to properly engage with the listeners. He'd share behind-the-scenes content, ask the audience to pick the next song, reveal personal details (beyond the DJ persona), and generally make the audience feel closer to him (and the radio station) much more so than by listening alone. Sounds fairly standard stuff nowadays from anybody in the media, but at the time, I went so far as to call him a pioneer! And so Colin was one of the many 'business' case studies that I used in the very early days of Embrace The Space. When I found the opportunity to turn him into a 'live case study' (explaining in person his social strategy) I jumped at the chance, and the 'rest is history'[121].

A true professional, I still wonder why he works with me. Obviously my banter keeps him amused.

Contact Colin at any time, especially if your enquiry is regarding any refunds or complaints about this book:
email: colin@comsteria.co.uk
twitter: @colinkelly

---

[118] I was tempted to insert a witty 'with the exception of' comment, but actually there's no better wingman than Colin. He's Iceman to my Maverick (although our heights would maybe swap around for that comparison).

[119] Oh how I wish that was just a white lie to exaggerate this book, but alas, we have indeed been called this, by more than one person, on more than one occasion!

[120] Deja Vu anyone?

[121] Colin absolutely hates the phrase 'the rest is history'. I added it just to annoy him.

More about Gary (as exaggerated by Colin).

What impresses me most about Gary is his ability to get the best out of any situation and his commitment to amazing customer service. I don't want to be accused of saying nice things in order to get a bigger slice of the proceeds of this book, but it's fair to say he is held in extremely high regard throughout the business community.

We seemed to hit it off when he would call into my radio show (he took part in various daft pranks) and was more than happy to make a prat of himself when required for mine and the audience's benefit! He's also a big sports fan and when he invited me along to the NSDesign 10th birthday party back in 2009, which was hospitality at a Glasgow Rocks basketball match, I was delighted to accept.

That night, Gary said a few words and was joined by NSDesign's very first customer, from ten years previously, who was still a customer all that time on, and who had travelled a few hundred miles to be in attendance. It was then I realised the positive impact a business could have, and since then, having worked closely with Gary for so long I've learnt so much from his approach to life and work. He loves to champion small businesses, and help them punch above their weight. He loves helping them get better results and I think one of the secrets of his success, and what makes our social media training so popular, is that it's much more than social media training. It's much more than 'marketing advice'. In fact, it goes right to the heart of what business is all about. It's about understanding people, treating them well and doing the right thing. People walk out of our course not just with extra social media knowledge but with an attitude that's going to enhance the way they live and work in the days, weeks, months and years ahead.

Contact Gary as your 'phone a friend' if you're ever on 'Who wants to be a millionaire' and get stuck on a Bon Jovi question:
email: gary@nsdesign.net
twitter: @nsdesign

More about Keith (as written by himself).

Absolute legend.

But seriously, I'm an illustrator and software developer who originally met up with Gary to discuss some business consultation for a fledgling game development company several years ago. We immediately clicked, mainly based on our shared love of Bon Jovi (contrary to what others have said, Tinder was not involved), and we agreed to 'Never Say Goodbye' and to keep in touch 'Always'[122].

The consultation was highly motivational and gave me a lot of food for thought, which inspired me to attend the Embrace The Space workshop. I was so impressed by Gary and Colin's engaging presentation, the wealth of information delivered during the workshop, and left the workshop buzzing with ideas to try out!

When Gary and Colin later told me they were writing a book based on the workshop, and enquired if I'd be interested in providing the illustrations, I jumped at the chance. It's been a privilege to be part of this amazing book (I'm allowed to say that, I've read it!), and as I've told them many times: 'I'll Be There For You'[123].

You can find more info on me and my work at www.keithatherton.com

---

[122] No more Bon Jovi song references beyond this point.
[123] OK, OK, last Bon Jovi song reference, I promise. Blame Gary, he started it.

Epilogue

how it all began

Embrace The Space: how it all began

Gary's version:

Rewind to 1999, February the 15th to be exact, and the birth of NSDesign. We'd actually been going a while prior to that, but this was the date that I registered the nsdesign.co.uk domain, and what is now considered our official birthday.

I say 'we' – back then it was just me. Most businesses do that don't they? They exaggerate their size fearing that if the client works out I'm just a one-person company I'll not get the work! Nowadays, I advocate celebrating the fact you're small, and all the positive values that are synonymous with smaller businesses. More personal, more caring, more ownership, more attention to detail, more compassionate, more human. I'm not saying that bigger businesses cannot be these things, but in the crowded, connected world in which we now operate, the big corporate brands realise that now more than ever we do business with people.

Anyway.....I digress.

For the first ten years of our existence, NSDesign could be pigeonholed as a Digital Agency. Primarily we designed and built websites (hence the 'design' part of our name) for anyone who would willingly pay us! Starting a business is tough, and it's hard to say 'no' to anybody willing to pay for your services. Looking back, I wish I'd said no to a good few of them, but that's for another book perhaps.

From web design came the natural progression into domain names and web hosting, and from there into the digital marketing world. After all, these same clients needed those awesome websites hosted somewhere, and then marketed to get the attention and traffic they deserved.

As our menu of services grew, so did our head count. We were never a big company, but by 2009 we had approximately a dozen bodies which comprised the team, some of them full time employees, some trusted freelancers, regularly contributing to the heavy workload which was essential to keep 'feeding the beast'.

We were also by then running a few digital training workshops on topics such as web design, search engine optimisation, and increasingly, social media. I took it upon myself to run most of them.

Back then it was still very new. Businesses still didn't understand it, or how they could take advantage of it. Most assumed it was an over-hyped fad, that Bebo would soon disappear, and there was no point in learning Twitter as only big celebrities used it. These assumptions weren't exactly wrong at that point, but those making them didn't see the bigger picture, and where it was all heading. Many businesses back then were looking for social media training for their management teams hoping I'd reinforce their beliefs and decisions not to invest in any of this social stuff. Wanting me to tell them not to bother with Twitter, or FourSquare, or Facebook (which at the time was mainly used by just college and university students).

They got the opposite. They got me on a mission to challenge them, inspire them, convince and convert them. Why? Because I passionately believed (and still do) that strategic use of social media can change businesses.

NSDesign's reputation as a champion of all things social grew. As did the demand to deliver wider training workshops on the related platforms and topics.

Three major events (which I didn't realise the significance of at the time) followed:

1. Ronnie McLaren from Business Gateway asked me to design and deliver an 'introduction to social media' workshop, for local businesses in Renfrewshire and Dunbartonshire. This was arguably a first across the country. The topic wasn't yet cool enough (or mainstream enough) for business support agencies to actually put money behind it, and upskill their local businesses. The sessions were an instant hit, and we were block-booked to deliver these on a weekly basis. Overnight we became a training company.

2. Laura Mills from the Renfrewshire Chamber of Commerce agreed to fund us to deliver a pilot of an 'advanced' workshop, taking things above the 'introduction stage' and giving businesses an intensive full day session, covering platforms, strategy, content and more. It wasn't based on 'hype', rather evidence – analytics, data and actual case studies of businesses we'd helped where we could prove a return on using social media. We called the session 'embrace the space'.

3. I hired Colin Kelly. I was already using him as a case study in the workshops, so it made sense to bring him in when I had the chance. I needed help to deliver what was now a sizable order book for our training sessions, and Colin was the perfect fit. Not just a natural at delivering workshops on his own, but a natural complement to me and my own style of presentation. The double act was born.

In January of 2010 I called everyone for a meeting which essentially had one thing on the agenda. I asked everyone the question: 'What are we "world-class" at?'. What followed was a colourful discussion where every aspect of the business was discussed, dissected, and questioned. We were great at web design, and the guys in the team were exceptionally talented, but was it world-class? We provided awesome customer service to our hosting clients, but was it world-class? We were developing some really cool and useful marketing systems, but did we truly believe nobody did it better than us?

We concluded that most of what the company did was great, but arguably not the best. With the exception of our training. It might sound big headed, but at that point, myself and Colin (some others too) genuinely believed that our training was exactly that. World-class.

Looking back it was extremely unfair. How can you be a world-class web design company when the world was full to bursting with web designers (every third person attending a Business Gateway workshop at that time seemed to be starting a web design company!). But with our social media training we were pioneers. We were delivering social media training to businesses before many others (I still argue we were the first!). And we were doing it in a way that seemed to really work. The feedback didn't lie, the attendees loved it, and more importantly, we loved delivering it.

It was just after that meeting that I decided to restructure the entire company. I won't bore you with the details, but the decision was made (in my mind if nothing else) to focus exclusively on the digital training side of things. It wasn't a hard decision to make. Far too many family sacrifices and lost time fixing servers until 4am, or weekends in the office with client design deadlines. Commercially, I was well aware that those other divisions while already competitive, were just going to get even busier. We were fast moving into a world where Google was giving away free websites and GoDaddy were selling domains for a pound! That's a hard space to make your own and return a profit. Plus, if I'm entirely honest, my heart just wasn't in it anymore.

I just wanted to get in front of people, and talk about social media and digital stuff!

Long story short, a buyer was found, who not only acquired NSDesign's web design and hosting services, but also the staff delivering them. I owe a huge amount to the team that supported me over the last 20 years, and I'm proud to say that not a single lost job resulted from the company restructure, with many of the original staff still in the same roles today. The end result was a scaled down, 'back to basics' company with a focus on Digital Skills and helping people develop them.

The Embrace The Space pilot was extended, adapted, and promoted to more audiences across the country. Colin and I continued delivering it from our Hillington offices (which conveniently had very nice training facilities), while numerous 'flavours' were created to better suit specific clients and sectors. Versions of the masterclass were created for the service industry, the education sector, the finance sector, the health sector, local authorities, housing associations, the engineering world, the sporting world and more. It has been adapted into workshops, seminars, webinars (lately, lots of webinars!), conference talks, keynotes, lunch and learn sessions, breakfast tasters, 1-2-1 coaching sessions and a whole lot more.

Colin recently challenged me on my claim early in this book; 'Have we really taken Embrace The Space to over 10,000 businesses over the last decade?' he asked. We then sat for over three hours reminiscing over just some of the sessions delivered across the UK. The numbers stack up.

Prior to 'lockdown' our most recent masterclasses were delivered from a brilliant training venue near our offices (sadly now looking like another casualty of COVID-19 and unlikely to reopen). A vibrant multi-purpose space which included go-karting, cafe, and conference facilities, there was also half a plane (yes, a real passenger plane) stuck to the side of the building which was a cool talking point and great #selfie spot! It was run by a social enterprise whose mission was, 'Empowering lives and fulfilling potential through care, education and opportunity'.

Their goals nicely overlapped with ours.

Embrace The Space (in all its guises) attracts businesses, business owners, and their staff all with one thing in common. They give a damn. We do too. Here's to giving a damn over the next decade, and as my dear departed Mother always said (so much that we engraved it on her headstone) – 'Keep Smiling'.

Colin's version:

When I answered the call from Gary ten years ago and first got involved in the early versions of what is now Embrace The Space social media training, I could never have imagined how successful and fulfilling it would be, and that it would have grown to become the beast it is today!

Part of that, of course, is due to the rise of social media itself and how it has integrated itself into so much of our lives and businesses. But that doesn't explain why our particular brand of training has thrived while so many others have come and gone. I think our success lies in the fact that, underneath the specific advice and insight around Facebook, Twitter, LinkedIn and now TikTok, YouTube, Instagram and more, is that at its heart, Embrace The Space is about an attitude.

There's an energy and positivity that runs throughout what we deliver (and I hope you feel it in this book too) and Gary and I passionately believe in the power of digital as a force for good in our lives and work. The businesses which attend our workshops get that too. While some might arrive in the room mildly (or sometimes entirely!) sceptical about it all, they quickly come to realise that in fact, success on social media relies on values such as customer service, listening, understanding your audience, innovating, and looking after your staff.

I remember a few years back, one of our participants had something of a light-bulb moment during the workshop. She'd arrived mildly unsure of how it could all apply to her business and unsure of whether 'technology' was for her. As the day went on, it clicked and she couldn't help but express the change she felt. 'Success on social media is actually about getting back to good old business values,' she said.

She was right. And that, in essence, is what Embrace The Space is about. It's the core message we reinforce throughout the course. It's what unites everyone who has attended Embrace The Space since it began. It's a community, an attitude, a belief.

We can make things better.

We give a damn.

① A ✗ 1920 ⟨1850⟩
② B ✗ 1690 1842
③ B ✓ 1960 1970
④ ⟨C⟩ ✗ 1951 1993
⑤ Dumbardcer ✗ 72 120
⑥ Mde ✗ 22 ⟨66⟩ ←
⑦ Fod. ✗ ⟨3. 5inch⟩ 4.5 ↙
⑧ ₺. 1.2 2.6
⑨ Women ←
⓪

① A →
② C ✗ ⟨S. 4⟩ 7.4
③ B ✗ 2.60 ₄₄.
④ D ✗ doohi. 8 . 12
⑤ B ✗ Danin Clem. —
⑥ C ✗ Meg Nya —
⑦ D ✓
⑧ B ± A ⟨Cut⟩ Sud
⑨ C ✓ Mount Tum
⑩ B ✗

Printed in Great Britain
by Amazon

46348117R00170